Flash Teams

The MIT Press's publishing mission benefits from the generosity of our donors, including Robert Pozen.

Flash Teams

Leading the Future of AI-Enhanced, On-Demand Work

Melissa Valentine and Michael Bernstein

The MIT Press
Cambridge, Massachusetts
London, England

The MIT Press
Massachusetts Institute of Technology
77 Massachusetts Avenue, Cambridge, MA 02139
mitpress.mit.edu

© 2025 Melissa Valentine and Michael Bernstein

All rights reserved. No part of this book may be used to train artificial intelligence systems or reproduced in any form by any electronic or mechanical means (including photocopying, recording, or information storage and retrieval) without permission in writing from the publisher.

The MIT Press would like to thank the anonymous peer reviewers who provided comments on drafts of this book. The generous work of academic experts is essential for establishing the authority and quality of our publications. We acknowledge with gratitude the contributions of these otherwise uncredited readers.

This book was set in ITC Stone Serif Std and ITC Stone Sans Std by New Best-set Typesetters Ltd. Printed and bound in the United States of America.

Library of Congress Cataloging-in-Publication Data

Names: Valentine, Melissa (Melissa A.) author | Bernstein, Michael S., 1984– author
Title: Flash teams : leading the future of AI-enhanced, on-demand work / Melissa Valentine and Michael Bernstein.
Description: Cambridge, Massachusetts : The MIT Press, 2025. | Includes bibliographical references and index.
Identifiers: LCCN 2025001994 (print) | LCCN 2025001995 (ebook) | ISBN 9780262049849 hardcover | ISBN 9780262383868 pdf | ISBN 9780262383875 epub
Subjects: LCSH: Teams in the workplace | Crowdsourcing | Online social networks
Classification: LCC HD66 .V353 2025 (print) | LCC HD66 (ebook) | DDC 658.4/022—dc23/eng/20250530
LC record available at https://lccn.loc.gov/2025001994
LC ebook record available at https://lccn.loc.gov/2025001995

10 9 8 7 6 5 4 3 2 1

EU Authorised Representative: Easy Access System Europe, Mustamäe tee 50, 10621 Tallinn, Estonia | Email: gpsr.requests@easproject.com

To the talented students who were true collaborators and made this research possible

Contents

Part I: Building Your Flash Team: Experts Are Everywhere, All the Time

1. Building Flash Teams 3
2. Experts Everywhere, All the Time 13
3. The Forgotten Power of Role Clarity 27
4. The Tactics of Hiring and Onboarding in a Jiffy 37
5. Get the Conditions Right, and the Team Behaviors Take Care of Themselves 45
6. Adaptation Is a Flash Team Imperative 55
7. Enabling Flash Team Adaptation through Software 63
8. Mobilizing Hierarchy for Dynamic Adaptation 75
9. Mobilizing Hierarchy as a Network for Change 85
10. Practice the Art of Collaborative Repair 93
11. Navigating Worker Voice and Client Voice 103

Part II: The Future of Flash Teams: Supercharging Your Teams with AI

12. Getting the Right Team in a Flash with AI Hiring 115
13. Designing Flash Teams with AI in the Loop 129
14. Using AI to Improve Your Teams 137
15. AI for Flash Team Simulations 151
16. Predicting Flash Team Outcomes with AI 159
17. Building a Healthy Ecosystem for Flash Teams 167
18. Conclusion: A Bridge from Here to There 181

Acknowledgments 191
Notes 193
Bibliography 205
Index 215

1 Building Your Flash Team: Experts Are Everywhere, All the Time

1 Building Flash Teams

To begin, Mark had nothing but an idea. Then, within a few weeks, the idea had become a working app—one that solved a major problem at his job.

He brought that app to life with a team of more than thirty designers, user researchers, and software engineers from around the world. You might guess that, to turn his idea into a functional, user-tested piece of software in just weeks, Mark had the ability to divert a top team from his company onto the project. But, no—there was no team at the outset. Instead, Mark started from scratch and assembled those thirty diverse experts as the project demanded them, each one joining within minutes in response to his call.

Mark is not a startup founder or a high-powered executive. If you push him on it, Mark will admit that he actually has no engineering or product background at all. He's a doctor in the emergency room, and he decided to create an on-demand team when he noticed a concerning but solvable issue at the hospital where he works: until the back doors of an ambulance opened, the emergency room staff had no idea what was coming their way.

Like many of us, he saw a problem and had an idea for how to solve it: "Surely we shouldn't be waiting until the ambulance actually arrives for the E.R. to spring into action? What if first responders could let the hospital know in advance what is coming in the ambulance?" Mark envisioned a mobile app that ambulance drivers could use to report trauma cases while en route to the hospital, and a paired wall display in the E.R. that visually displayed incoming cases.

Mark didn't stop at the idea, though—and this is where the story of this book begins. Instead, using tools and techniques that we developed in our research labs at Stanford University, Mark assembled and led an on-demand team that produced a fully functional, user-tested prototype of the app and a paired display for the hospital, all within six weeks.

Mark's a doctor, so he didn't know how to hire or manage software developers on a new product. He also didn't know what to do when the feedback on his first prototype revealed that he would need to dramatically redesign the application. Or what to do when he realized that he needed to ensure compliance with HIPAA around medical data privacy. Or even what to do when he realized that he needed marketing materials to help funders and users know about the app. But still he began, using an approach that we developed to quickly adapt and collaborate with a global team of experts to achieve his goal.

On-Demand, Computationally Powered Teams

We call these on-demand, computationally powered teams *flash teams*, and they hold lessons for every manager and for the future of work. Until now, problem-solvers like Mark were accustomed to working with teams that are overly constrained, resistant to change, and slow to learn. We recruited Mark as an entrepreneurial user who wanted to learn flash teams, and like him, we now similarly aim to show you in this book how to take advantage of a global remote workforce and artificial intelligence (AI) to create teams that are the exact opposite: flexible, rapid, and adaptive. Flash teams:

- Recruit exactly who is needed, within minutes, from a global remote workforce
- Pivot rapidly when contingencies inevitably arise
- Apply AI to help recruit the right people, evolve, and manage the team

The two authors of this book are professors at Stanford University, where we've brought together the bleeding edge of management science with computer science to create opportunities for flash teams like Mark's to achieve these goals. Melissa Valentine is a management scholar: she studies what makes teams work in the digital age. Michael Bernstein is a computer scientist: he builds platforms that bring people together. We were both young assistant professors when an enterprising PhD. student named Daniela Retelny Blum heard separate research talks from the two of us and realized that we really ought to be talking to each other. Those initial conversations launched us on a path that has reshaped how we think about the future of work, and we have a hunch that it will change your perspective too.

The flash team from Mark's story, as well as the tools and skills that he mastered, are rapidly emerging as the future of teams and teaming. Gone are the days of static organizational charts and staffing based on the manager's own rolodex. AI, remote work, and online platforms are transforming how teams work. You can recruit any expertise you need from a global online network: an on-demand, on-the-spot expert at the exact moment that you need their help. You can right-size each person's involvement: some of those experts offer a second opinion or a moment of brainstorming, while others join as full-fledged team members for a sustained collaborative effort. You can craft an organizational chart that reshapes itself and adapts based on data.

A decade of our research has exposed the aging, creaky old infrastructure, assumptions, and adages about how to hire, how to onboard, how to collaborate, and how to manage. Lessons from flash teams invite us to reconsider: what can we create today? How can we manage teams more effectively? And what role do new technologies play in enabling these teams of the future?

This book is a story about flash teams and the cutting edge of management. It's also a story about the lessons that we learned as we built some of the world's first flash teams, including the software that powers them. But this book isn't an ad for the software we built to enable flash teams. Instead, this book distills the lessons that any manager can learn about what it means to hire, assemble, collaborate, adapt, manage, and learn in an age of on-demand, remote, global experts and AI.

Visions of Better Teams

As assistant professors with our eyes on tenure, we focused on our research. That research was written up in the *New York Times* and led to presentations to thousands of people over the following years. As our work reached larger and larger audiences, people kept coming up to us afterwards and telling us what they would build if they had flash teams themselves. The ideas were varied, inspirational, and just plain cool. These people's stories inspired us to write this book.

An employee from the Minneapolis Department of Motor Vehicles described their idea to use a flash team to develop a new digital system for one of their main pain points in managing appointment times. A female entrepreneur suggested that flash teams could help female founders address well-known disparities in venture capital funding by making it cheaper to get to first prototypes. A therapist from Australia imagined creating flash teams of mental health professionals to help with different situations, overcoming the problem of the great physical distances and limited mental health workforce in Australia. Graduate students envisioned convening teams of immigration lawyers and experts to help people who were getting stuck at the airport because of travel bans. One of our founder friends, after a successful exit with her first company, envisioned how a flash team would enable her to start to prototype her new consumer packaged goods from home. After Valentine[1] appeared on a podcast called "The Future of Everything," CEO Anna Shpak in Germany reached out to say she had created her own flash team during the pandemic to create a software system for tracking environmental regulations and compliance.

The visions came from large companies, too. Valentine gave a talk to executives at a professional services firm called EY, where leaders immediately expressed excitement about creating flash teams of auditors to do their complex and distributed audits. We met someone from inside Google who had basically bootstrapped a similar idea, assembling on-demand teams from among the available internal consultants in her department. We received an email from a contact in the military who saw the opportunity to experiment with flash teams models drawing together teams from their internal workforce. A vice president at J.P. Morgan talked about how venture capitalists could help their founders use flash teams to bring down the cost of creating the first minimum viable product. In fact, one of our first collaborators worked at an advanced technology lab at Accenture, where they created their flash team to build a workshop portal that integrated with Accenture's enterprise systems and branding.

This movement isn't restricted to just our research: since we began our work, we've seen other companies and communities also innovating in this space. We worked with the founders of Gigster, who were creating flash teams of designers and engineers convened and guided by smart software systems. We met the founders of HourlyNerd (later wisely renamed Catalant), which created flash teams of MBAs to create business plans. We met founders of a community called Artella that curated a large network of animators, designers, artists, and engineers that had coordinated software that allowed them to create movies together. People can see the potential of what's starting to be possible now, and we want to help you understand what is possible and how you can be a part of it.

When discussing flash teams, people quickly recognize their potential applications. It's inspiring to hear how both technical and formal leaders envision using on-demand teams of experts across various contexts. They readily identify the problems they could solve with the right opportunity, skills, and resources to lead a flash team.

What Flash Teams Mean for Organizations and the Future of Work

You can win a Nobel Prize by explaining why flash teams might spring into existence. Economist Ronald Coase did.

In the 1930s, Coase posed a now-famous question that founded an area in economics known as "theory of the firm."[2] Why, he asked, do we have organizations instead of just hiring whoever we need out of a marketplace of contractors? Coase foresaw, decades before we wrote this book, that a single global marketplace could give you access to whatever expertise you need. He reasoned that, to the extent that markets are efficient, it should always cost less to contract work than to hire someone. But—aha!—Coase reasoned, the literal cost of the work is not the only cost that you bear. You have to go search for a good person in the marketplace, and you need to spend time securing a contract with them. These search and contracting costs aren't zero, because they take you time and effort. These costs can, in fact, be huge. So, Coase argued, we have organizations because it's cheaper to have ongoing employment contracts with a huge group of employees than to search and contract for every new thing you need done.

Today, those costs have shifted with internet and data technologies: searching and hiring is much less time, effort, and money. That shift is the fundamental reason why flash teams could not exist before and can exist now. Suddenly, search can be nearly free and instantaneous: online marketplaces provide search features that match you with workers given just a description of what you need. Contracting can *also* be nearly free and instantaneous: these same platforms allow workers to advertise their rates, and the platforms provide contract guarantees. The platforms offer application programming interfaces (APIs), which allow employers to write programs to search, contract, and hire at blazing speeds. When search and contracting are cheap, Coase's theory tells us that people will begin to use marketplaces where they previously used organizations.

We are of course already seeing these shifts. Management scholar Jerry Davis of the University of Michigan has been reading these tea leaves for over a decade. In *The Vanishing Corporation*, he writes about the following key trend:[3]

- Between 1996 and 2015, the number of American corporations listed on US stock exchanges declined from 8,000 to a bit over 4,000.
- In 2015, "The combined workforces of Facebook, Yelp, Zynga, LinkedIn, Zillow, Tableau, Zulily and Box were smaller than the number of people who lost their jobs when Circuit City was liquidated in 2009."[4]

Davis argues that the larger reduction in traditional corporations is related in part to newer digital technologies such as online labor markets and related organizing models such as flash teams. Large sprawling corporations such as Sears, US Steel, and General Motors made sense under old technological assumptions. But the changing technology landscape is changing the nature of organizations. As Coase's work suggests, the costs that made it natural to bring people into organizations permanently may be shifting to favor alternative forms of organization such as flash teams.

As is common, the first actors to move on this insight and trend have been individuals, small organizations, and startups. They are scrappy and open to new ideas. We have personally seen startups draw on online labor markets for business plans, designs, and engineering. It can be a compelling picture: imagine your small local business elastically growing to ten or more contributors when needed in crunch times.

Slower though they may be, larger organizations are recognizing this opportunity as well. Freelancing platform Upwork advertises that Microsoft, Airbnb, Bissell, and Nasdaq all have enterprise contracts with their platform, enabling them to hire from Upwork's freelancers. Our own employer, Stanford University, has such a contract. The enterprise contract that Stanford lawyers hammered out with Upwork lawyers ensures that Stanford remains compliant with California labor laws as it hires freelance work through the platform. Our executive education program, our alumni office, and several other professional and administrative groups at Stanford have hired freelance workers through this effort.

Out of Reach?

While people have inspiring visions of flash teams, they also face a clear barrier: they don't know how to go about it. Valentine was recently on a work retreat talking with some mid-career professionals who were incredibly impressive, thoughtful, and innovative in how they approached their organizations and careers. On her turn, when she talked about flash teams, one of these CEOs, who had been in the newspaper for her innovative approach to funding a coworking space, said, "That's really cool . . . but I wouldn't know how to do that." We kept thinking back to that moment: it had not occurred to us that tactical understanding might be a barrier for people using flash teams—even among people who in general liked to try new ways of organizing.

Likewise, a friend of ours was complaining about her custom-designed website not integrating with her Shopify or her Toast point of sale software. She struggled to carve out hours each week to try to figure out this problem. Our immediate response was, "There is no way you should be spending your time on that! There are experts who can help." We showed her how to search an online marketplace for the first time. We quickly found profiles listing people within her budget with experience with Shopify, Toast, and custom websites. She was shocked: "How did I not know about this? How have you not told me about this before?" This is how we learned that, unlike most professors, we should talk about our work at dinner parties.

Because flash teams have been part of our lives for a decade now, we can readily put them to use, but there's a missing instruction manual: there's a gap between people's visions of flash teams on one hand and the skills and confidence needed to actually run a flash team on the other hand. Even though not everyone needs a large, cross-functional on-demand flash team like the one we described at the start of the chapter, everyone can pick up some new tricks and techniques from flash teams.

Flash teams have even changed our own lives. Today, Bernstein is working on a research project developing a new social media platform. On-demand software engineers have been part of that project nearly since day one, filling in his Stanford team's experience and time gaps. Another research project involves collaboration tools for online artists. So, Bernstein and his PhD student began hiring online artists to playtest the tool every week. Flash teams have helped us learn new software tools, fix bugs, and implement features.

We wrote this book to help. We want to help you, like Mark the doctor who wanted to use flash teams to save lives at the hospital, become an expert in this new form of management. This book represents our sense that flash teams are a key to the future of work and that they exemplify key capabilities that every manager can learn from and apply, no matter the size and maturity of their project, their company, or their teams. A globally networked workforce can be a powerful lever for your ideas.

Software: The Flash Teams Foundry

Flash teams may be powered by online labor markets, but you can't just bring people together and then assume that you'll have a successful project: you need to coordinate and collaborate. Over our decade of work in this space, we found that flash teams coordination software is what really supercharges flash teams. Traditionally, teams have mostly collaborated offline: you'd tap your teammate on their shoulder, you'd see each other in the lunchroom, or you'd meet in person regularly. But, because all the flash team coordination and management happen through the internet, those interactions aren't available. Flash teams aim to turn this lemon into lemonade: since the interaction is all happening online, software can support every single leg of the flash team's journey. In this book, you'll hear us describe how we use software to intelligently hire, design, and manage flash teams in ways that you never could offline. Many of these tools draw on recent advances in artificial intelligence.

Because we were among the first in the space, we had to build this flash team coordination software ourselves. Throughout this book, you'll see us refer to our software, called Foundry, because we had to create it in order to enable flash teams. You'll see how we used Foundry as a layer on top of online labor markets to enable many flash teams superpowers: hiring quickly, pivoting rapidly, designing and redesigning the team structure, and selecting team members using AI. In our research, some of these tools went by other names too, like Huddler, Dream Team, and Hive. They are all a suite of tools. We'll call them all Foundry in this book, to keep things simpler.

Since we built Foundry, the major companies that use flash teams today have also created software tools that echo many of the same goals:

- Catalant developed tools for creating and supporting collaboration for teams from among a curated marketplace of business consultants.
- Gigster, A.Team, and Manuel Pistner's Flash Hub all created internal tools for automatically staffing teams and managing their projects.
- B12 created software for team assignment, collaboration, and many teamwork processes.
- Artella created tools for collaboration on the team's creative assets.

Some of these tools are used internally only; Gigster, for example, uses its tools to support its internal flash team staffing. Google DeepMind organizes AI researchers into strike teams and frontier teams. Other tools are available open source, like B12's tool called "Orchestra" that supports collaboration. You can build or buy, as your organization's requirements dictate.

But if you're looking to just dive in and get started, you can make it happen without any special software. When we started building flash teams, we collaborated with the team at Accenture Technology Labs. One of their talented engineers, Taurean Dyer, realized they could approximate our software using freely available project management tools. He recently told us,

"What was revolutionary about Foundry was that it was like the blueprint. And I saw that you could take that blueprint and apply it to so many different combinations of work tools, and that's why it was really impactful."

At the end of his work leading a successful flash team, Dyer reported to the company's leaders that he could use other platforms to mimic parts of Foundry's functionality as a base, and displayed images of Basecamp, Trello, Freelancer, Accenture's internal Digital Talent Broker platform, Sharepoint, and Box. We agree with his conclusion: you can get very far with these tools as long as your teams use them appropriately. Software changes fast, but as of our writing, Asana or GitHub Projects can help you track tasks, Slack can help you keep everyone communicating, and even plain old spreadsheets can help with hiring sometimes. If you've really adopted the flash teams mindset, you can make it happen with these off-the-shelf options and without learning new tools. Then, as you settle in, you can start exploring more advanced or custom software like we did, to supercharge your efforts.

As we proceed through the first half of the book, we'll share our advice on what software we think you ought to use. We'll ground it all in our Foundry software, and what it enabled us to do. Foundry itself was research software, which means that it was good enough for our deployments but not a product that can stand up to widespread use. So, we'll share the software that we would use today.

Then, in the second half of the book, we'll turn a corner and show some of the software superpowers for flash teams that aren't widely available in products yet. These superpowers include automatically building teams based on your description of what you want, adjusting the team management over time based on observations on how the team is proceeding, enabling early warning systems that predict when a flash team might not work out, and presenting tools for team members to self-organize.

If you start building with flash teams today, our argument is that you are going to be incredibly well positioned to take advantage of these incoming superpowers. In the short term, you can either use freely available general tools today, or dive into some of the tools that other companies have started publishing. In the medium term, if you're building a larger organization around flash teams, you might follow B12 and Gigster's leads and build some custom tools internally to help. And in the long term, we'll paint a picture of what is coming down the pike with software.

Regardless of the infrastructure you use, flash teams will change the world. They will be used to create, to build, and to inspire. They will offer opportunities to entrepreneurs who need rapid expertise, to large businesses that seek to be nimbler, and to anyone else who has an important problem to solve.

2 Experts Everywhere, All the Time

Pat Petitti needed a team. His client was closing their retail stores but wanted to figure out how to keep selling their brand's beloved toy truck in a new model each year. As the founder of Catalant, which uses technology to form, manage, and empower on-demand teams of consultants and business professionals, Petitti turned to his company's network to convene the team he needed. He found:

- An expert who had been an associate partner in retail at McKinsey, the management consulting firm,
- An expert who had worked at Toys R Us on corporate development, and
- An expert who had worked at Amazon on the supply side.

The perfect team for this problem. The client hired that team, which then knocked it out of the park—to the point where the client asked Petitti, "Can we just keep the team on to manage all of the execution of the work as well?" They rehired the team to do just that. Those three experts exceeded all expectations—despite never having met before, and never being in the same room as each other.

Understanding flash teams starts with this simple mindset shift: *experts are everywhere, all the time*. In the traditional US labor market, we have been trained to adopt a mindset of expert scarcity: there are very few experts your company can hire, and if you need another one, it will take weeks or months of time and piles of red tape to hire them. Understanding flash teams means turning that perspective upside-down to a mindset of expert abundance: that whatever the expertise or skill is that you need, it's probably available, and you can probably get access to it quickly.

In the same year that we published our first flash teams study, it took a typical firm in the United States 14 to 25 days to fill a new hire.[1] Our research asked: What if those 14 to 25 days could become 14 to 25 *minutes*? Suddenly, leaders could start making different decisions. And if those hires could offer deeper skills than what firms could get through a traditional hiring process, those decisions will start looking very, very different indeed.

We've both demoed this idea in our classes. Valentine would introduce a flash teams lecture by saying to the student teams, "You need to get a professionally sourced team logo by the end of this 80-minute class." She would then show them how to search and hire in an online labor market that had millions of contractors. Going from idea to an expertly produced team logo within a single class period seemed crazy to the students at first, but in the years that Valentine did this exercise, every team of students easily hired a graphic designer who created a team logo for them (using class funds) before the end of the class period.

Bernstein does another demo. He decided to use Cameo, an online marketplace where anyone can hire actors and celebrities to record short custom videos, to hire actor Chris Diamantopoulos to record a personalized message for the class. Chris played billionaire investor Russ Hanneman on HBO's show *Silicon Valley*, and Bernstein hired him to record a video comparing his fan interactions on social media versus Cameo for the class. It was ready the next day.

These demos, which convene only single experts, are intended as fun illustrations of the speed with which experts can be found, but in this book we'll show you how the truly exciting potential of these technologies comes when you can convene *teams* of specialized experts.

Online Labor Markets

We can start with a deep dive into online labor markets as a source of experts for flash teams, and then distill some key takeaways for managers. Let's get started with a brief tour of these online labor markets. Think of online labor markets as website platforms that connect workers and employers. Workers post their resumes and their availability for work, and employers post projects. Workers apply to work on projects, employers select a worker, the two agree on a wage, and away you go. While many bells and whistles can be added to the marketplace, including the ability to track time, choose between hourly and fixed-price contracts, demonstrate skill through scores on platform-provided tests, and assign ratings to workers, the basic recipe is about matching workers and employers.

These online marketplaces relate in some ways to the gig economy platforms that you are probably familiar with, such as Uber or DoorDash. But modern online labor markets provide access to far more varied kinds of expertise for many different kinds of projects. Here are a few examples:

- The Upwork online labor market, which has over 12 million registered freelancers, connects clients with a diverse range of experts, including freelance writers, graphic designers, web developers, translators, virtual assistants, marketers, and many more.
- Fiverr specializes in creative expertise including graphic design, writing and translation, digital marketing, programming, video editing, and music production.
- Catalant, featured at the beginning of the chapter, curates an online labor market for business consultants.
- A.Team organizes a team-driven network of tech developers, product managers, designers, marketers, data scientists, and senior operators.
- Artella, an online creator community created by ex-Pixar employees, hosts freelancers with the skills to create Pixar-quality animated films.

How do these online labor markets work? They offer features that allow millions of freelancers and clients to offer and apply for jobs, negotiate and monitor work contracts, and transact internationally compliant payments, all at scale. Typically, the platform provides a template contract, a set of rules, and dispute resolution procedures. When you create a project, you describe it and specify the expertise you require, the rough hourly or total compensation for the project, and any other constraints such as level of experience, language skills, time zone requirements, and the level of independence you expect. If your company has specific riders for contracts—for example, required non-disclosure agreements—platforms can often facilitate that as well.

Once you post your job, workers will apply online. This typically happens within hours. We also recommend searching the platform and explicitly inviting a few well-suited candidates to apply to the job, since the best workers may not otherwise see your project. Workers will vary in their backgrounds, locations, and how much they charge. Their applications may

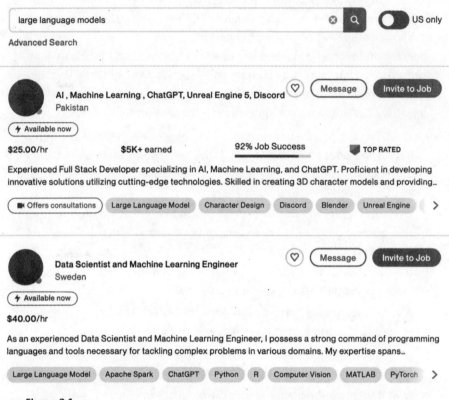

Figure 2.1
Upwork's search interface allows you to search for any expertise and find workers who match that expertise.

respond to the specific job requirements or show off their relevant portfolio elements.

Key Services That Help with Online Marketplaces

One of the key services these platforms provide is a set of signals to help you make an effective decision in who to hire. The most important signal is typically a *reputation score*, similar to a five-star rating that you'd see on Yelp or Amazon. Many different statistical and client feedback signals can enter into this score, making it the platform's secret sauce. It might integrate ratings from previous clients, or factor in whether the projects were completed successfully; it might more heavily weigh feedback from clients who have been on the platform longer and are better at comparing contractors; it might automatically adjust to focus on more recent work rather than ancient history. More on ratings in chapter 11. In the meantime, platforms make lots of other signals available as well. So, if you search for an AI engineer, you'll typically see:

- Their name, hourly rate, and rating,
- The number of hours they've logged on the platform,
- A selection of feedback reviews from previous clients,
- Their resume, and
- Platform-assigned badges to qualify the worker in a specific area of expertise or as a top-rated worker on their platform.

We encourage you to try making a client account on one of these platforms and searching around for expertise in your area. You might be surprised by what you find.

The Experts You Can Find in These Global Networks

The diversity of skills that can be hired through online labor markets can seem overwhelming at first. Fear not. We will take a tour through the online labor market mall, laying out the kinds of work that we can (and can't) commonly find through these labor markets. It's important to emphasize that not all of these platforms yet have the required components for the flash teams software that we describe in this book—for example, some cannot enable hiring through an API (a software interface that lets you hire using a program instead of using a website), which means that our flash teams Foundry software can't hire them automatically yet, and you'll need to manually post the job and hire on the website yourself. However, this tour should give you a taste of what current and future platforms may offer. We'll tell you about our various experiences working with these kinds of on-demand experts.

Software development. The first stop on our tour is software engineering. Strong software engineers are all over online labor marketplaces. Name any modern software platform, or nearly any ancient software platform, and the marketplace has someone who can work with it. Upwork, Gigster,

CloudDevs, We Work Remotely, Workana, Freelancer, and others have many fine-grained categories of software experts.

We have been fortunate to collaborate with many talented software engineers in on-demand and extremely helpful ways over the years. As a simple example, Bernstein often works with Stanford undergraduates who are extremely skilled—but who are not yet professional engineers, and who do not yet know modern software toolkits. Expert engineers from Upwork can help. In one project, Bernstein and a team of undergraduates were developing a tool that required a React web application, but the students were still earning their sea legs in programming with React. Bernstein hired an Upwork contractor who had hundreds of hours of experience with React web applications to support the development team. This skilled engineer, named Lokesh Bansal, performed code reviews to help teach the undergraduates good style and engineering practice, and he took on features and bugs that were urgent or beyond the current abilities of the team. He answered questions and gave advice. Over the course of several months, he was one of the core pillars of the group's success. Bernstein also learned from him, brainstorming together to think through particularly confusing parts of the design.

Hiring in this area highlights one of the major requirements of using an online labor market: you need to know what you want. Telling a software engineer to "make me an app" is no more informative than telling an architect to "make me a house." We keep learning this lesson. More than once, we have posted a software engineering project that we quickly learn is too open-ended. "No, wait, I wanted you to implement the algorithm that *I* told you about, not one that you think is better!" "Wait, why did you add a login system?" The more details you can specify in the contract, even to the level of specific example behaviors or user interface mockups of the software, the better. But describing what you want in enough detail is hard! More on this in chapter 6, titled "Adaptation is a Flash Team Imperative."

Design. The next stop in our tour is design. Often upstream of software development, if you need user interface design, logo design, graphic design, or any other form of software-based design, you are likely in luck. Many skilled designers offer their services through platforms such as We Work Remotely, Upwork, and Freelancer.

Once, a group of designers helped Bernstein quickly learn that one of his ideas was not actually very good. He had wondered if social media might be

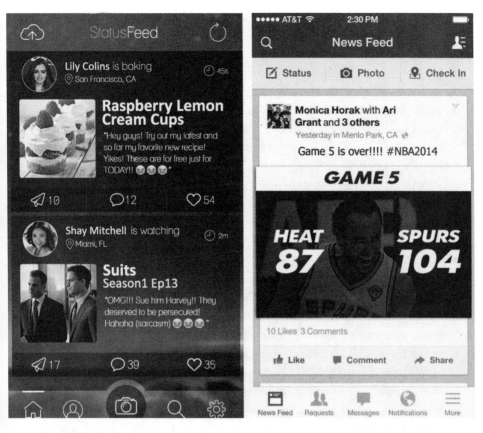

Figure 2.2
Designers can quickly create design mock-ups to help test out creative ideas. Bernstein sourced these designs to test an idea about social media posts that surrounded television shows.

more engaging if users could develop custom templates for certain posts. He thought, "What if users could create social media posts that were themed around the TV show they were commenting on, or the NBA show they were commenting on?" He wrote out these concepts and then hired three designers off Upwork to create visual mockups of the concept. He quickly got back some very solid visions of what this feed might look like.

The mockups were vivid enough that Bernstein immediately saw that the idea was maybe not as compelling as it had seemed in his head. On one hand, this is disappointing news. On the other hand, it's a huge win: he learned in just one day that his idea needed to be shelved, rather than after spending months building it. Sometimes success is about the projects that we choose not to do, and the Upwork designers were key in accelerating that decision process.

Business, finance, and strategy. In addition to engineering and design, you will also need business skills to create impactful teams and solutions. Online labor markets also connect you with experts in accounting, finance, procurement, strategy, supply chain management, and in many other disciplines. Depending on your project, you may not need or be able to afford a full-time employee dedicated to these issues, or you may need a bit of time from someone who is a deep expert in an area where your organization only has a generalist. You will easily find these experts within more general markets such as Upwork, and in more specialized markets such as Catalant.

As an example, a start-up founder we consulted with needed a business model for her consumer packaged goods company and was intrigued by the flash teams model. Finding an available part-time CFO with expertise in consumer product goods seemed like too specific a profile. But she got an immediate hit on an online marketplace: a Columbia MBA who advertised himself as a fractional CFO with expertise in consumer packaged goods. Within a day, she had an hour-long meeting where she described what she needed, and within a week he made her the financial model that she used to test the viability of her product and market.

Creative: writing and video. The creative sector has established many footholds in online labor marketplaces. Platforms such as Upwork, Cameo, Dribbble, and others showcase portfolios and enable you to hire artists, animators, and producers. We have worked with many flash teams including creative experts to create animations and videos using flash teams. One of the first teams we asked to create an animated video telling the story of one of our senior colleagues at Stanford—Terry Winograd, whose hair is eerily reminiscent of Albert Einstein's—building a computer in his garage when he was growing up. We hired a director via Upwork, who then brought on four other roles: a scriptwriter, illustrator, animator, and voiceover artist. Despite never having worked together before, this team met; developed a script, a storyboard, character design, and background design; animated the

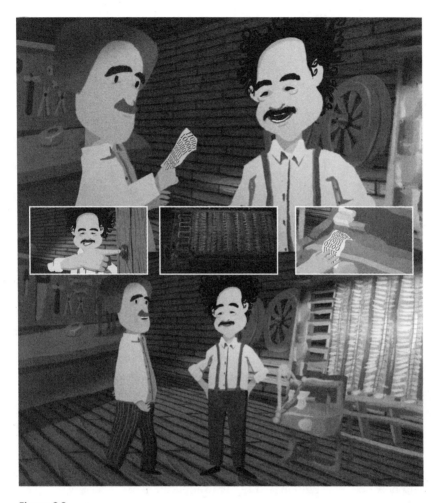

Figure 2.3
Flash teams created a short video animation about Terry Winograd in a matter of days.

Figure 2.4
Flash teams quickly created marketing materials when Mark, the ER doctor, realized he needed to communicate his idea to funders and users. This is a screenshot of one of the videos showing the functional GPS feature.

characters, then added music and voiceover; mixed the audio; and edited the final video, all in a matter of days. The resulting short animation was impressive.

Likewise, by pulling together a similar team, Mark, the doctor in our introduction, created a marketing video for a tablet application they had developed to alert hospitals to incoming ambulances. The team quickly created an animated marketing video that conveyed the use of the system and how doctors would make use of the application.

Of course, creative work was also where we first learned that "you get what you ask for, but maybe not what you intended." Bernstein was working on a new research project, an email application that granted Upworkers valet keys to specific subsets of your email to help you manage your email overload.[2] The team created a video demo of the application and hired an online actor from Voice Bunny (now called Bunny Studio) for a voiceover narration of our video script. Our task description explained that this video would be accompanying a scientific paper about the project and asked for a voiceover "like a documentary about a fascinating topic." Unfortunately, the voiceover that came back, while clearly from a competent voice actor, might be best described as an advertisement from a radio jewelry salesperson, and not a scientific documentary.[3] We worked with the artist to better match his talent to our vision of what the ad needed to do.

Artificial intelligence and data science. In a sense, artificial intelligence created the first online labor marketplace. Amazon launched its data annotation service Amazon Mechanical Turk in 2005, calling it "artificial artificial intelligence." Since then, on-demand human data annotation services that label data to train artificial intelligence models have grown into an entire industry, with platforms including Appen, Scale AI, Clickworker, and Samasource. Be especially careful with paid data annotation—it is especially easy to underpay workers or engage in wage theft in this kind of work, since it can be difficult to correctly estimate how long tasks take, and difficult to distinguish whether errors are due to worker error or actually due to your unclear instructions.[4] But these platforms, and their equivalents inside most large tech companies, are absolutely critical to generating the labeled data that these companies use to train their artificial intelligence systems.

You can go farther than that, though: you can also hire artificial intelligence experts to build, train, and deploy your AI systems. Traditional organizations needed to spin up entire AI teams to build these algorithms. Now, you can find an expert to help engineer it for you, even if your organization doesn't have the expertise in-house. You will still likely need to prepare and clean your dataset—again, no free lunches here—but this is about as close to an AI consultancy as you're likely to get.

Other expert professionals we have hired through online labor markets through the years:

- Product managers
- Quality assurance
- Instructional design
- Customer support
- Sales, marketing, and search engine optimization (SEO)
- Language translation
- Administrative assistance

When we say, "experts are everywhere, all the time," we really mean it: an astonishingly wide variety of professional expertise is available on these platforms.

What's Not Yet Possible with Online Labor Markets

If nearly any job that can be done over a computer will be in these markets, the inverse is also true: if it can't be done over a computer, it's less likely to be found online yet. For example, you're less likely to see a metalworker, or an HVAC professional, or an arborist, on these platforms. Folks would be more likely to consult local listings by going to Yelp or similar platforms.

This isn't a firm boundary: The TaskRabbit platform offers this kind of service, though it's constrained to local experts given the requirement that someone actually show up at your home or work. Likewise, we might think of online crafting marketplaces like Etsy as a kind of online labor market. However, Etsy is framed more as a shop than as a labor market: meaning, I can buy things on Etsy, but it's less straightforward to hire one of the creators on Etsy to take on a contract position in my organization. Overall, it's just harder to create digital-first organizations that have substantial requirements for in-person collaboration or physical materials that need to be shipped around. It's doable, just difficult. For now, hiring local help is outside the domain for which we recommend flash teams.

A final note: There are several platforms that are essentially online job boards, including Indeed, LinkedIn, and Monster. It is possible to draw on these platforms to hire experts for flash teams, but they are not your best bet. Work on those platforms is focused on traditional employment rather than flash teams. In addition, the platforms themselves don't natively support contracting or payment, which are a big advantage of the platforms devoted to creating flash teams.

"Experts Everywhere" Is About More Than Just Online Labor Markets

These first examples are all about how quickly you can search and hire from online labor markets, but the mindset shift to recognizing that there are *experts everywhere, all the time* is much broader than that. Calling on expertise may be as simple as looking within your own company. When studying a data science team at a San Francisco tech company, Valentine observed them creating many mini-flash teams on the fly. The core project team called in a data scientist assigned to another team who was an expert on causal inference, then another who was expert on the company's data model, and then a third with specific expertise in user interface design. All of those collaborators were full-time employees deployed on other projects but they were able to temporarily join forces with this core team to help apply their expertise to specific problems.[5]

Notice the same pattern in a series of patient case meetings we observed at an academic cancer center.[6] A doctor and a project manager would figure out all of the experts who might be helpful on a complex patient case—oncologists in other specialties, pain management specialists, dermatologists, nutritionists, social workers, clinical trial administrators, financial services, or palliative specialists, for example—and would convene the relevant group for a few minutes to discuss each patient case. The experts for each specific case might be different, but this integrative care program showed that different groups of specialists (i.e., flash teams!) could be flexibly convened to consult on complex patient cases at these short, focused cross-functional meetings. For those meetings, the cancer center staff were the ones convening the bespoke sets of experts for each patient case, but we also often see patients and families find and coordinate teams of experts through their own informal work.[7]

You can think of secondments or job rotations through this lens of *experts everywhere*. In a secondment, a company temporarily redeploys an employee to a new position that asks them to focus on a new project, client, or skill set. Notably, the employee can keep their same salary and benefits and return to their original job. As an example, the software company Atlassian sponsors secondments for some of their employees. They temporarily redeployed a product marketer into a marketing analytics team, which she and they found to be an invaluable learning experience.[8] Meta, the parent company that makes Facebook and Instagram, also features a "Hackamonth" sabbatical system that rotates their engineers temporarily onto other teams.

We all now live and work in a highly specialized and expert economy, and our internet and communication tools make it possible to find and draw on these experts like never before. Whether you searching for relevant experts in the formal labor markets, or in a company's knowledge management systems, or through a quick post to your social media accounts ("Hey hivemind, recommend a good contractor?"), you are likely constantly searching for and creating constant moments of expert collaboration. As professors, we get a lot of requests to offer our ideas or expertise, and thanks to our research, we have a unique vantage point. All it takes is a bit of a nudge to more aggressively reach out to the resources that are available in your business life.

In fact, A.Team founder and CEO Raphael Ouzan believes that people are highly motivated to share their expertise on problems and projects they care about. He was surprised by how many senior leaders applied to join the network of experts fueling their on-demand teams. Many of these leaders felt they had mastered the corporate game and saw no clear path for further advancement. Instead, Ouzan noted, they wanted to work on projects of their choosing, with collaborators they respected. By attracting so many experts eager to contribute to meaningful projects, the A.Team network grew faster than Ouzan had imagined.

That's the broader vision: if you think of experts as being everywhere, the lessons from flash teams can help any manager of any project, no matter how they're defined. You've got a deep bench of talent. Use it.

3 The Forgotten Power of Role Clarity

It is day two of filming a spy thriller in Bangkok, and disaster has struck. A critical piece of equipment—a camera crane needed for a key action sequence—malfunctions just as the crew is about to film a high-speed chase through the crowded streets. The crew has never met before and has only started working together, but the director urgently needs solutions and ideas. The cinematographer, just flown in from Switzerland, quickly assesses the situation and proposes a workaround using handheld stabilizers. The grip team, led by a seasoned expert from Thailand, hears the idea and figures out how to adjust their setup to accommodate the new plan. The lighting crew, anticipating the change, brainstorms how to adjust their rigs to ensure the shot still captures the desired effect. Together the cinematographer, grip lead, and lighting lead discuss how these changes impact camera angles and choreography for the action sequence.

What do flash teams have in common with film crews? That question sounds like the lead-in to a joke, but it actually highlights a core lesson from flash teams. To wit: from the start, the best collaborations come when experts are deeply specialized but still know how to integrate their efforts with each other. The ability to specialize and then integrate well with other specialists in a team is called *role clarity*, and it is the main engine of coordination for flash teams, film crews, and other teams that convene temporarily for complex work. When experts are very clear on their specialized tasks and responsibilities, they can focus on their highest-value contributions and trust that their equally focused and specialized team members are doing the same.

What is remarkable about film crews as an organizational form is that they often come together and accomplish high degrees of specialization *and* integration even though many people on the crew have never actually met each other before.[1] Relative strangers show up on the scene and immediately know how to work together. Before they even start talking, they know who is responsible for what work, who has the authority to make which decisions, and who hands off work to whom. That's role clarity. And it's remarkable to see the power of role clarity fueling active dynamic coordination among temporary groups.

The Forgotten Power of Role Clarity

We often forget about role clarity as a strategy because traditional teams have learned to move along without it: they can accomplish this degree of specialization and integration because members grow familiar with each other over time. Through repeated interactions over months or years, I learn what I can expect from you, and you learn what you can expect from me, allowing us to collaborate effectively. And even in the worst case, you learn over time how to work around my foibles to get your work done. This process is a reason why constant team turnover can be so devastating to traditional teams' performance and well-being. For flash teams to succeed, we cannot assume member familiarity.

How, then, do on-demand sets of experts become a functional team? The power of rapid hiring from online labor markets might sometimes land us straight into Odd Couple territory, full of awkward and out-of-step collaborations. Group projects with randomly assigned group mates are often a special brand of terrible experience in college. Why would the outcome be different here? What tools and techniques allow flash teams to collaborate effectively?

The answer, as we note above, becomes much clearer when we realize it's not just film crews that succeed despite constantly changing membership. Disaster response crews such as firefighting teams convene on site when a disaster strikes and may have never worked with the other teams' firefighters that they are expected to collaborate with. Within an emergency ward at a single hospital, ER teams are constantly rotating, and yet they succeed.

Film crews, disaster response crews, and ER teams all establish very high levels of role clarity. Like the specialized group in the movie *Ocean's Eleven*, every person knows their *role*—the expertise and job function they are expected to bring to the team—within moments of arriving, and how their role fits into the overall role structure (and chain of command) of that scene. As people take on their role and get to work, they can start to function as a team and they can coordinate impressive collective work.

In some industries, this kind of role clarity emerges after decades of the industry working out best practices. Our examples of health care teams and film crews do their work within industries that have benefited from long periods of evolution where roles became well defined and understood across the entire industry (doctor, nurse; or director, gofer, gaffer, grip). When an industry is experiencing rapid change, such role clarity can be harder to achieve. Editor Lisa Pinto told us about such a change in college textbook publishing: for decades, roles were well established, but the sudden shift to ebook publishing and online content delivery introduced significant confusion. Traditional roles overlapped with new digital roles, creating a period of uncertainty that lasted for years. We see similar challenges today with the introduction of AI across various industries. However, even in fast-paced, evolving industries, role clarity can be an achievable goal for flash teams. We'll talk throughout this book about how flash teams software can facilitate role clarity by providing dynamic documentation, a single source of truth, and other support systems that help streamline and define responsibilities more quickly.

Role Clarity and Role-Based Teaming for Flash Teams

The goal of role clarity in temporary teams is clear: effective, adaptive role-based teaming among people who may not have worked together before. Imagine a patient in crisis in a hospital emergency room. A group comes running. The first person immediately secures the patient's airway while a second person begins chest compressions. A third person runs into the room and starts an IV. A fourth person is standing at the head of the bed calling out to everyone that they're about to move the patient from a gurney onto the bed. As the situation stabilizes, all of these staff members say hello and introduce themselves to each other. They have never met before. And yet they each had role clarity to know how their expertise and responsibilities fit into that life-saving moment.[2]

Collaborative performances like this illustrate the power of specialized roles and expertise. People did not introduce themselves and did not need to discuss what exactly needed to be done and who was going to be able to do it. Because of their role clarity, they immediately knew what they were responsible for. The first nurse could focus on chest compressions while trusting that it was someone else's task to secure the airway. During her research on temporary teams in ERs, Valentine saw groups create even more role clarity during a crisis by assigning responsibilities based on the order in which people entered the room.

Zooming out of these singular moments, you can see that this kind of coordination based on role clarity is the motor of the whole bustling emergency room, where flash teams of doctors and nurses who have not worked together before manage to treat hundreds of patients per shift.

The point here that seems remarkable is that we as a human society have developed so many specialized roles for so many kinds of problems—and that simply by understanding their roles, groups of strangers can show up to a situation and, in a moment, know how they personally can contribute and what they can count on each other for. The ER is an extreme case, but once you start noticing roles and role structures, you'll see the power of role clarity for enabling many kinds of collaboration.

It was this magic of role clarity that made flash teams really start to work. Bernstein had been trying to bring together on-demand experts from Upwork, but wasn't sure how to get them to coordinate and not step on each other's toes. Valentine had been studying role clarity as the key to rapid team assembly in hospitals. One of us had a lock, and the other had the key. With this understanding of roles and role structures, we started to see that each flash team project we were designing seemed to have the same set of roles: we'd have a UI designer, a UX designer, a front-end developer, and a back-end developer. And they seemed to consistently accomplish their tasks in roughly the same order, collaborating in fairly consistent ways across the projects. Even without a ton of experience in software engineering projects at the start, we could learn how to be savvy clients of these teams based on understanding the general roles and role structures involved.

Step One: Build from the Roles Up

Based on this understanding of role clarity, the first step in creating a flash team is to begin by specifying the roles. When we bring someone into a flash team, we emphasize their role: "You are the user interface designer for this feature." "You are the front-end software engineer and will need to coordinate with the back-end engineer." "You run quality assurance—share any issues that you find with the front-end engineer."

Roles are often defined by area of professional expertise: you might be a documentation writer, or a QA engineer, or a financial analyst on the team. Defining the role structure means making sure that everyone in the flash team is told their role as soon as they show up. Don't just bring people together and ask them to work it out—someone, probably you, should tell each person their role. It's best to do so when hiring, so that people know what job and set of relationships they are stepping into. When we built our Foundry software for convening and coordinating flash teams, we structured each team into a series of roles (e.g., a designer, a user experience researcher, and two software engineers). For each of those roles, our software used an API to hire someone out of the Upwork marketplace.

Next, you need to specify how roles should interact with each other. "You are the front-end engineer responsible for the user interface implementation of this application, and you will need to coordinate with the back-end engineer to make sure that data get sent to and saved from the user interface correctly. You should call on the user interface designer whenever you have questions about the details of the UI specification." In other words, you need to draw the team's organizational chart for the relative strangers to show up and enact.

Structuring the *roles* does not mean structuring the *tasks*. Almost the opposite: the point is that, if someone understands their role, they can take direct ownership of coming up with the tasks that they need to complete. In fact, you don't need to micromanage someone who understands their role and their relationship to other roles. You may need to still set overall direction, like deciding which features to build or prioritize, but roles should help the team members know how to divide up the work and integrate their efforts.

Here's an example of how we would author a complete flash team using roles. We would decide the needed roles, and enter those roles into our flash teams Foundry software, which hires people to fill each role. To help establish role clarity, we would include this information in the onboarding and other elements of the UI:

- Goal: this flash team will create a single-page website for the *Flash Teams* book, describing the book to a business audience. The website should

make the case for flash teams by opening up the hood to show how the website itself was created by a flash team.
- Roles:
  - Marketing manager: directs the overall flow and content of the website, coordinating and overseeing the other team members
  - Writer: creates the content for the website, including excerpts from the book and testimonials from business leaders
  - Graphic designer: creates logos, graphics, and the overall visual layout of the website; produces not only the overall mock but also individual image assets
  - Engineer: implements the website from the graphic designer's mock once the marketing manager has approved it; sends any questions to the graphic designer for clarification; hosts the website once implemented
  - Book Authors: provide feedback and approvals to the marketing manager on the website design and contents
- Deadline: Two weeks

With that information, each worker knows what the team's goal is and what their own role is within that picture. The leader has created a role structure to convene the needed experts and begin to establish role clarity.

Role Foraging

Yet role clarity is not a passive state. Certainly, it helps when everyone has a good sense of what all roles do. But even with a shared sense of the basic role structure, there are a lot of details and contingencies that have to get worked out to arrive at role clarity. There are active behaviors that team members will engage in to help the shared sense of the role structure turn into actual role clarity.

An engineer at Gigster, one of the companies we collaborated with on our flash teams research, explained the problem this way. He said, "At the start of a project, the team gets together on Slack and you're supposed to start a pretty complex software project right off the bat. But at first, you don't know these other guys. Let's say someone's title is 'front-end engineer.' Does that mean they know the same programming languages I do?

Do they follow the same practices that I know work well, like when it comes to commenting on code or writing solid documentation? Some engineers have very different ideas of how to do things and who's in charge of what because they may have learned software development at [a big technology company], or at a scrappy startup, or maybe they're totally self-taught."[3]

How do flash team members and managers create the needed role clarity? Something we observed in all our flash teams was that when new workers show up, they'd begin engaging in a behavior that we call *role foraging*. Role foraging is when people seek out any information that would make clear what their role on the team ought to be, and what the expectations of them are.[4] They immediately and actively started asking questions that were relevant to their specialized roles and exactly what they needed to do.

Each worker's foraging strategy will be shaped by their expertise. Valentine had a funny experience learning how powerful people's roles will color what they think is required of them. She had hired a designer to help her with a simple newsletter. She needed, at most, a few ideas on how to make an email header. Instead, the worker delivered an over-designed, interactive PDF. In looking at the exquisite design—and Valentine's chagrin at what she had unwittingly ordered—a UI designer colleague of Valentine's laughed and quipped, "Designers gonna design."

In the joke is a useful point: UI designers have a specialized expertise and toolkit that they expect to use. Once you've got them in the design role, it will be hard to get them to do anything less than design. And the useful insight for flash teams is that UI designers will show up and immediately start asking the same basic set of questions in order to figure out what they need to do. The questions they ask are very different from the questions a front-end developer asks. After all, developers gonna develop.

Failing to use role structures effectively leads to errors that are amusing at best and destructive at worst. We have seen this firsthand, by investigating logs of flash team interactions from Slack. If there is not enough clarity, new members will forage around for clarity on their role, seeking any information they can get their hands on to make clear to them what they are supposed to do. In fact, this experience isn't even limited to flash teams; it's often the case that the most challenging part of starting a new job is *figuring out what your job is*. Without enough role clarity at the start, there can be reams of unnecessary extra messaging in public channels, extra meetings, and confusion. On the other hand, if the team is over-structured with an inflexible workflow, it cannot respond to contingencies or pivot when better opportunities emerge.

We think that as you start to envision flash teams for yourself, you'll start to see many different roles and role structures that are relevant in different situations. When people become experienced in an industry, they develop an intuitive understanding of what the relevant tasks are and who typically is going to do them. Writing has authors, editors, illustrators, and publishers; marketing has brand experts, visual designers, content producers, and advertising experts; remember even *Ocean's Eleven* had each member contributing specific skills and roles.

Using Software to Reduce Effort and Increase Role Clarity

With many flash teams, we have the benefit that all the work is being done through online collaboration platforms. When work happens online, you can leverage the ongoing trail of work, decisions, and documentation to support role clarity. If you don't, you're going to see constant exchanges like this one we observed:

- Chris: "Is there a search feature for date range?" Mike: "Yep, it should be in the docs."
- Another day. Chris: "We need a delete or hide function; is there a route for that?" Mike: "Yep. I mean it's in the docs, there's not much to add."
- Another day. Frank: "Has the stats been implemented on PIA?" Mike: "Yep check the docs."

We don't really mean to laugh at poor Mike's frustration at having to constantly tell people to go read the documentation that already holds the answer to their questions. It is the truth of role foraging: a lot of the great detail on what *exactly* people should do will be in that ongoing trail of documentation.

If you build a large enough flash team, you cannot rely on everybody knowing everything, and so you must rely on documentation to maintain a single source of truth. Still, up-to-date, helpful, searchable documentation is not a given. Sometimes the software systems can help automate this process, especially now with all of the meeting transcriptions and summarizations that generative AI tools offer. But even with that help, teams still often need a relentless insistence on keeping high-quality documentation going, with consistent practices around naming, tagging, dating, and identifying all documentation in a reasonably consistent format.

It can be hard, but it is possible. One inspiration for understanding the role of documentation in flash teams is location-independent organizations (LIOs), such as GitHub, Atlassian, and Dropbox, which are large, mature companies that have no physical offices. It's a coordination feat to keep 500 remote workers contributing in sync even though they are rarely in the same place. Jen Rhymer of University College London did her dissertation on LIOs and took this on as a puzzle—how do they coordinate without being in the same place?[5] What management structures and practices make this possible? Rhymer found that their success depends on their workforces documenting their processes extremely well.

Some of the LIOs took a fully asynchronous approach to coordination. These companies did not have meetings, and they did not expect people to work regular hours to be able to talk to each other and keep in touch. What they did have, what was fully necessary for these teams, was very thorough and up-to-date documentation. They needed a rich trail of decisions that had been made, including mistakes, alternatives considered, and a very up-to-date current state of work. This meant that when someone stopped working, another team member in another time zone could log on to start their work and quickly understand what had happened, why, and what it meant for their work of the day. The best practices that made this asynchronous approach to complex coordination included:

- Single source of truth (SSOT) documentation: the organization has a centralized, authoritative repository of data or information that all teams and systems rely on.
- Auditable decision trails: this trail documents not only the final decision but also the alternatives, changes, rationale, discussions, inputs, approvals, and any relevant data or evidence that contributed to that decision.
- Empowered autonomous decision-making: establishing a culture where people trust that they are expected to make decisions autonomously, as long as they document them and are able to go back and revise them if new information emerges.

These LIOs push the limits of asynchronous coordination using documentation. They have learned to equip their teams with the accumulation of knowledge developed during the course of all their many projects, including all previous decisions and outcomes. And they have learned that for their teams to operate effectively, that information needs to be easy to search, access, and understand. LIOs have come up with increasingly sophisticated software capabilities (e.g., global search) and management practices (e.g, rituals, cadences) to help. Imagine a flash team assembling and getting to work with that kind of documentation available. Imagine the role clarity that can quickly be foraged with high-quality documentation and easy, global search by a new team member excited to contribute to the new project. That's the vision for flash teams.

4 The Tactics of Hiring and Onboarding in a Jiffy

Taurean Dyer's clients were accustomed to fast-moving teams. But even so, they could not keep up with how fast he assembled a flash team and built a new system for them.

Dyer's clients were an internal group at Accenture, where he was an engineer in their advanced technology labs. They had commissioned him to assemble and lead a flash team to build them a new platform for organizing client workshops, which needed to integrate with Accenture's enterprise software systems and branding. He did so, bringing on roughly thirty experts across a series of flash teams to lead design, implementation, and testing of the workshop portal, all completed within a few weeks.

One of the clients later told Dyer that his flash team had completed the system faster than they would have been able to onboard the first person had they instead hired anew to build the workshop system. And, the client said, Dyer and the flash team had done it at one-eighth of their expected cost.

If the heading of part I is that experts are everywhere, its subheading ought to be that experts are anytime. One of the most startling implications of these global online labor markets is just how quickly you can hire. When Daniela Retelny Blum, the PhD student who led our foundational flash teams research, reflects on her experience building flash teams, it was this speed that stood out. She recalled, "The coolest moment by far was having an idea and having it brought to life in record time. The fact that we could come up with an idea for a mobile web application or an online learning platform and have it completed by a team of experienced experts in a day felt like we were truly living in the future."

But there are different practices that help to drive on-demand hiring to success. Hiring quickly happens to be something of a professional research interest of ours, so here we have some pieces of concrete advice, learned from experience and from many other leaders in this space.

The Basics: Hello, Nice to Meet You. You're Hired

One of the superpowers of online labor marketplaces is just how quickly you can hire. If you've got a clear and competitive job post, you can get offers from some of the world's top experts in an area within *minutes*. How is this possible?

These platforms are large, many with thousands or millions of available workers. That global reach and size is key to flash teams' unique ability to hire so rapidly. With hundreds or thousands of qualified candidates for your job, you will likely start receiving applications within minutes if your job post is clearly described and well priced. In practice, depending on your level of urgency, you may want to wait a day or two to collect applications before moving forward. Or, as we'll describe later in this chapter, you might have some automated guidelines for who is above your bar to hire, enabling you to quickly hire the first qualified person who applies.

You'll create a post on the platform to describe the role and the project that you are hiring for. You'll need to specify the expected length of the job, how much you're willing to pay, and how much experience you need the worker to have. The platform then takes over and begins sending your job post to qualified workers. You can search a list of available contractors and invite some to apply to your job, and the platform may advertise your job to contractors itself as well.

Typically, we will then use workers' ratings on the platform (more on this in chapter 11) and a review of their portfolio and previous feedback to filter down to a few candidates. We tend to do some old-fashioned interviewing at this point in order to compare those top few candidates. Then, pick one, send the contract offer through the platform, and you're off to the races!

What's remarkable about this process with flash teams is just how quickly it moves. As we will describe later, by pre-vetting workers, our Foundry software was able to complete this entire process from posting to hiring within a median fourteen minutes. Imagine the impact on your team's nimbleness and flexibility if you have confidence that you can bring in nearly any expert within fourteen minutes.

Getting Started with Smart Job Postings

To hire quickly and well, you need to be able to create effective job postings. Hiring *can* be a repetitive and tedious process. Someone has to write and post lots of job descriptions, someone has to sift through the many resultant applications of varying relevance and quality, and someone has to vet promising candidates. And hiring *quickly* can seem incredibly risky, like tying the knot before the first date. What if they don't show up? What if you don't get along?

As you know, hiring well is one of the most important things you do in building a team. We've met others working on flash teams–related ideas who have discovered similar challenges and strategies. Roger Dickey, together with cofounder Debo Olaosebikan, built Gigster into a company that offered their clients flash teams of on-demand, fully remote, and data-driven experts. Dickey told us that when they first posted a simple website advertising vetted engineers on demand, the offering went viral and they scrambled to keep up with demand. They also quickly learned that one of their main challenges was helping all those interested clients hire good, effective individuals and teams.

If you start a job posting on the Upwork market today, you will immediately be using smart automation, perhaps without even noticing what's happening. The job posting page will ask you for a headline but list several tips and examples above the text box. Advance the page and you're asked to indicate the job category (e.g., web design, full-stack development) and select three to five required skills among those that they immediately display for you (e.g., web design, javascript, html). Within seconds of use, you're into functionality that is deeply data-driven based on the millions of projects already completed on Upwork.

We've visited Upwork's offices in Mountain View, California and met with the data scientists and engineers behind the job posting functionality. They've learned from millions of posts that a key factor in project success is how well clients scope and communicate the work, not just the quality of the contractors. Upwork's data shows that well-crafted job posts by clients are as crucial to successful project outcomes as the contractors themselves.

The next several pages help you scope the role or the project (e.g., Under 30 hours? One-time? Fixed price? One month?). You input preferences for the kind of freelancer you want to hire: Expert or novice? Preferred location? Preferred language? Again, it's a deeply-data driven functionality even though to you it involves just picking from a menu.

This might be the smartest job posting system you've ever worked with. It makes you better at hiring because it helps you scope and communicate the role or project clearly and think about all of the relevant characteristics for any expert you're looking to hire.

Maxx Metti, the lead AI engineer at A.Team, another company in this space, described their vision and work to reduce every challenging or tedious aspect of the hiring process for their clients. He emphasized to us the potential of automating or assisting key aspects of the hiring process, likening the ease with which they could help their clients to an "autocomplete" function. Once you start to understand the underlying repetitive tasks, they can start to be structures on which you can accumulate data and learn about what works best. Clients can reuse their own job posts, and learn across many projects about what works and what kind of hiring leads to successful projects.

Hiring well is also incredibly consequential to a healthy society, because it is how people get access to opportunities. It's useful to see where automation can help but also where you personally need to pay close attention and make important decisions yourself. Two well-known examples from Amazon highlight the risks of online platforms and automation in hiring. In one case, an algorithm intended to streamline hiring discriminated against women applying for technical jobs because it was trained to find applicants who were similar to Amazon's current engineers, who were mostly male.[1] In the other case, automated systems fired Amazon delivery drivers without considering their real-world challenges such as access to delivery sites.[2]

In short, you will have a lot of help in thinking through and communicating the work you're needing to hire for. You post the job, and depending on the marketplace, numerous experts can see and respond. As with most opportunities in this book, one of our best recommendations is to give it a try!

Hiring Models: Open Call vs. Vetted Panels

Knowing that you can be equipped with a smart job posting system that helps you anticipate needed skills and desired scope of work, you can now think of flash team hiring according to two different models, depending on the marketplace you are using and your goals.

The first model might be called the *matchmaking* model, in which the platform completes the hiring autonomously: you say what you want, you wait a brief period, and the platform produces a worker who is available and ready to start working according to your terms. This model is familiar to users of gig economy platforms such as Doordash and Uber: you request a worker, and the platform takes care of the rest.

Matchmaking models are fast, but they do introduce risks. Just like Tevye's daughters in *Fiddler on the Roof*, you don't have direct control over who you're going to get matched with. All you can do is describe what you want, and then hope for the best. As clients on platforms such as Amazon Mechanical Turk have found, however, hoping may not be enough: workers who are the fastest to take the job can be scammers. Such workers might have built computer scripts to automatically detect new job posts, and automatically take the job, no matter their fit for it or their intent to do the job well. Such scammers are few in number, but have an outsized influence because of how many people they can harm. However, if the platform algorithms are effective and weed out these scammers, matchmaking hiring can be done within minutes. Going from a submission to a contract in minutes can be startlingly empowering.

The second model might be called the *application* model, in which you receive a pile of applications to your position, and you choose who to hire. As with Upwork, each application may come with many attendant details about each applicant. The platform may even recommend the strongest candidates to you. It may also recommend that you interview your top candidates before hiring them.

Applications invert the tradeoffs: they are slower and more work, but you have more control over who you hire. Often, if the platform can narrow it down to three top candidates, it is in your best interest to manually review all three. It needn't take long. Perhaps you're more willing to take a candidate who works during your work hours but is more expensive over someone who is cheaper but whose hours don't overlap yours; perhaps you are willing to take a risk on a promising candidate who has fewer items in their portfolio. The power is yours.

One strategy that we have developed is to use applications to vet a pool of qualified candidates, then use a matchmaking model from there. When we recognize that we are going to have a repeated need for a type of expertise, we use an application model to create a vetted panel of workers who we trust to take on jobs within the sphere of expertise that we need and who have agreed that they are interested. We then use the "open call" automated matchmaking model.

For most of our flash teams deployments, we used a similar approach by building custom software. We created curated and vetted panels of experts for different roles. "Vetted" meant they understood who we were and the kinds of projects we were offering, and we knew that they were interested, aligned, skilled, and wanting to work on team projects. Based on these vetted panels, we created in our Foundry software a digital hiring hall of sorts. The groups of vetted experts would receive messages about the team role we were hiring for, offering a first-come first-serve position in the flash team. The experience is not unlike buying concert tickets online. Workers arrived in the order in which they expressed interest, and had a window of time to review the job and its timeline before accepting or passing on it. Once a worker accepts, they begin working.

It took time to create these vetted panels of experts who were then ready and available on demand to join a flash team and start contributing. We had a whole team helping with that process for some of our deployments (cue an especially hearty shout-out to Alexandra To, Michael Kim, Corey Garff, and Maxine Fonua). But if that takes too much time for you, you can rely on platforms' built-in ratings and features. For example, Upwork offers paying clients the ability to tap into its pool of highest-rated workers. Some larger organizations offer vetted on-demand experts in what they call a "talent cloud" where you can reliably do the matchmaking, open-call model.

Curated Pools of Experts

Similar to our approach, the Gigster team introduced above used smaller testing and screening tasks to create curated pools of experts who were ready to join a team. They hired several people for tryout tasks, then offered more involved engagements to those who were the best fit and most successful. Dickey said that without these tryouts, the available expert pool for staffing new flash teams was often more prepared and aligned with the projects at hand. Our friend, a marketing leader, Sarah Brown similarly said that her company will hire three or four designers, pay them to create graphics, and then hire the person whose visual they liked the best if there is an ongoing engagement.

Pat Pettiti of Catalant described a related strategy for quickly assembling on-demand teams of business experts. Catalant has curated a vibrant market of such experts, but Pettiti says they also need to regularly check in with the network to see who is still active, interested, and available for this quick team staffing model. With their curated market of vetted experts, Pettiti imagines even real-time displays during client meetings that show clients some of their possible team members.

Similarly, Metti of A.Team described the importance of deeper and more customized interviews, evaluations, and onboarding processes for people working with on-demand hiring. He learned that a main challenge in helping match clients with teams was anticipating the variability in working styles between clients and external hires. For example, he had seen a large legacy firm with a formal style hire a few experts with relevant expertise in generative AI but who had only worked in scrappy start-ups and struggled to match the more formal style of the client. Metti helped A.Team gather more detailed expert profiles including factors such as management experience, autonomy, and adherence to guidelines.

These hiring approaches range in terms of how hands-on they are and when the hands-on effort happens. You can, of course, also hire a hiring manager to hire on your behalf. If you have enough consistent need to hire, you can hire a sure-fire, top-rated contractor who you trust and task them with reviewing applications to build out your team.

The smart job postings and different hiring models can really change the game when it comes to assembling teams to solve problems. In one of our research studies, we found that flash team leaders using our hiring hall software were able to hire exactly the expert that they needed in a median of fourteen *minutes*.[3] As we said at the start of this section: compare that to the typical hiring pipeline for a firm in the United States, which is 14–25 *days*.

Hiring the Right Team in a Flash

Up until now, we've focused on how to hire an individual worker from the platform. But there is much more that's possible—and critical—to a flash team's success. You don't want a bunch of individual contractors; you want Ocean's Eleven: a team that works well together. To assemble a traditional team like this, you'd shuffle through your rolodex of possible contributors and contact them one by one. But because flash teams are recruited through software, we can be smarter. Much smarter.

We want to automatically recruit not only experts who fill our needed roles, but also with an eye toward availability, how much we've worked together, time zone overlap, diversity, or any other recruiting goals we care to set. Each of these team hiring goals is an objective for the flash teams assembly engine. And you are likely to care about many of these hiring goals at the same time. Luckily, combining multiple goals under uncertainty like this is one thing that AI such as the flash teams assembly software is quite good at. That's what chapter 12 will help you do.

5 Get the Conditions Right, and the Team Behaviors Take Care of Themselves

At 4:35 pm on a weekday afternoon, the doctors, nurses, and assistants in the City Hospital Emergency Department sound like members of a sports team playing a fast-paced competitive game, shouting to each other their positions and availability: "I got it!" "Mine mine mine!" "Over here, I'm open!"

A nurse calls out: "Who's got Jones?"

A doctor yells back: "I do!"

Nurse: "Lab says you have to reorder all of her tests."

Moments later, another doctor calls out: "Who has Reyes? It's time to 'P.O. challenge' him."[1]

Another nurse replies: "He's mine."

Attending: "P.O. him. Then he can go."

This rapid communication helps ER team members coordinate and prioritize their actions in providing emergency care to the many patients for whom they share responsibility. This fast-paced teaming—real-time coordination to carry out interdependent work—indeed has much in common with sports teams, but instead takes place among highly trained professional knowledge workers who have, for the most part, not worked together before, and whose shifts only partially overlap in any given day.

We've talked a lot now about role clarity and automated ways of hiring experts, which are essential to how flash teams work. But it is also key to remember that flash teams are, well, *teams*.

Teams, as social groups, develop their own group-level dynamics. Getting shoved onto a team that doesn't work well together can be one of the most painful experiences in your career. Of course, the flip side is also true: more and more of the impactful work we do comes from teams rather than individuals, and effective teams can be some of our most fulfilling work experiences.[2] It ultimately depends on who's there, how you structure yourselves, how you treat each other, and how you work together.

Of course, flash teams are also a special kind of team. They're a kind of *temporary* team. Temporary teams are an increasingly common way of structuring work across various industries, like in-person ad hoc project teams. Temporary teams are interesting because their members are relative strangers, but they succeed only as those members engage in active and prosocial coordination together. Team members must fulfill their specific roles but also engage in prosocial teaming behaviors such as proactively noticing problems and notifying others, asking or answering questions, taking time to collectively integrate perspectives or priorities, or stepping in to do each other's work.

Psychologist Amy Edmondson of Harvard Business School has called these teaming behaviors "risky" and "prosocial," meaning team members will look at the social environment to decide whether to engage in those behaviors.[3] What is so interesting about temporary teams is that the conditions that typically motivate such behaviors in traditional teams, like strong social identity or longstanding relationships, are not present in these ephemeral, one-time engagements, raising questions about how temporary teams achieve effective coordination.

In this chapter, we'll talk about how to set the stage for these behaviors and for team success. Because of the on-demand, ad hoc, and ephemeral nature of flash teams, a lot of important team design decisions can and should happen before you press "play" in hiring teams (not just individuals) and in onboarding and launching teams.

Onboarding and Launching

During one of our visits to the headquarters of Gigster, we also asked cofounder Olaosebikan what he thought his most important lesson learned was from running Gigster. His reply: "You have to get the launch right."

Olaosebikan explained how, in the early days of Gigster, they would convene a team quickly, but then all the team members would show up with different preferences for platforms (Slack or Teams, Google Drive or Dropbox), spend days figuring out how to set up and integrate their various software tools, figure out their collaborative working processes, and then finally get to work. This is a huge problem if it's repeatedly happening over hundreds of teams in a company that is advertising flash, on-demand development projects. So, Gigster got better at the launch phase of teaming.

The important work of the launch is making sure everyone understands the team's purpose, goals, timelines, tools, communication plans, and decision-making processes. It's more easily said than done. But here is another place where the computational nature of flash teams can be a boon. Although much of the creativity and excitement of flash teams is around the newness—creating something new with a custom group of experts—the basics of a new project launch can be encoded into tried-and-true project management tools and communication checklists.

Why encode the launch into the software? To understand this, we need to dig into what happens if you don't. New members of flash teams are primed to hit the ground running. They will immediately start by trying to figure out exactly what their role is and how they fit into the bigger picture. They are foraging for information, sniffing out anything they can find. This is the *role foraging* that we talked about in chapter 3—it describes figuring out your role in the team.

The solution to this poorly designed launch can lie in the flash teams software. Because it recruits everyone and has a notion of what their roles are supposed to be, it can substantially improve this launch without interrupting you or other team members. We achieved this by building an onboarding module into our Foundry software. In the onboarding module, flash teams software first introduces workers to their role, responsibilities, and collaborators. Figure 5.1 illustrates how this works. It begins by showing workers the broader context of the flash team: What are the tasks that have already been completed? What is coming up?

It then shows the worker their own task, and how they fit into the current plan. Since the flash teams software is role-based, it knows which tasks each role was assigned, so it can call the worker's attention to the first task for their role. By drawing the worker's attention to their own task, it helps focus them on what they should be looking to work on.

Clicking on their task, workers get even more details. What are the deliverables of the task that they're contributing to? Who else are they expected to collaborate with on this task? Where are the materials they might need for their task, like any upstream results or data? Where should they put their deliverables?

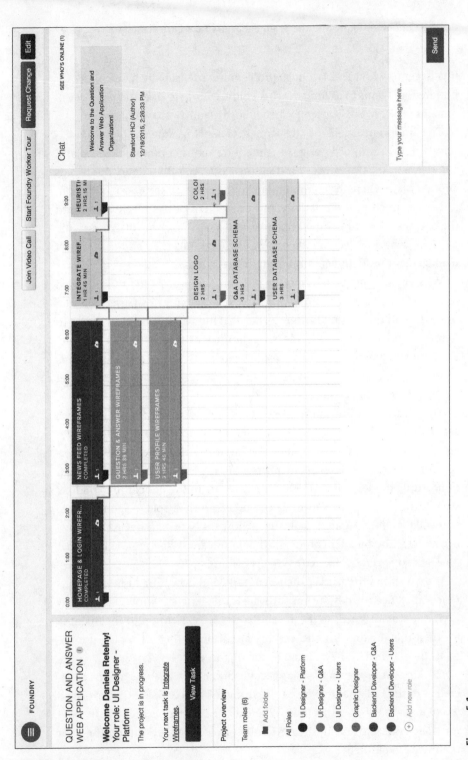

Figure 5.1

Foundry's timeline is role-based. It shows the worker their own task, and how they fit into the current plan including interdependencies with other

ADD TASK

HIRE

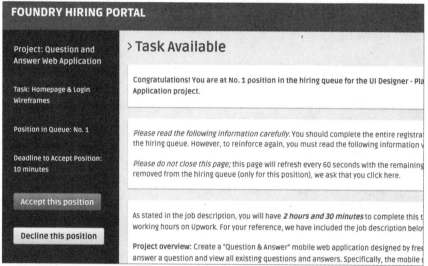

ONBOARD

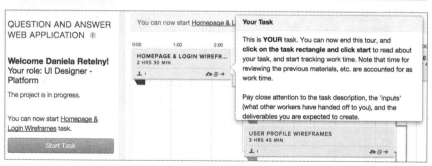

Figure 5.2
Foundry's onboarding helps workers understand the specifics of their work within the context of the team's work. It also includes a tour of the overall platform to familiarize users with its features.

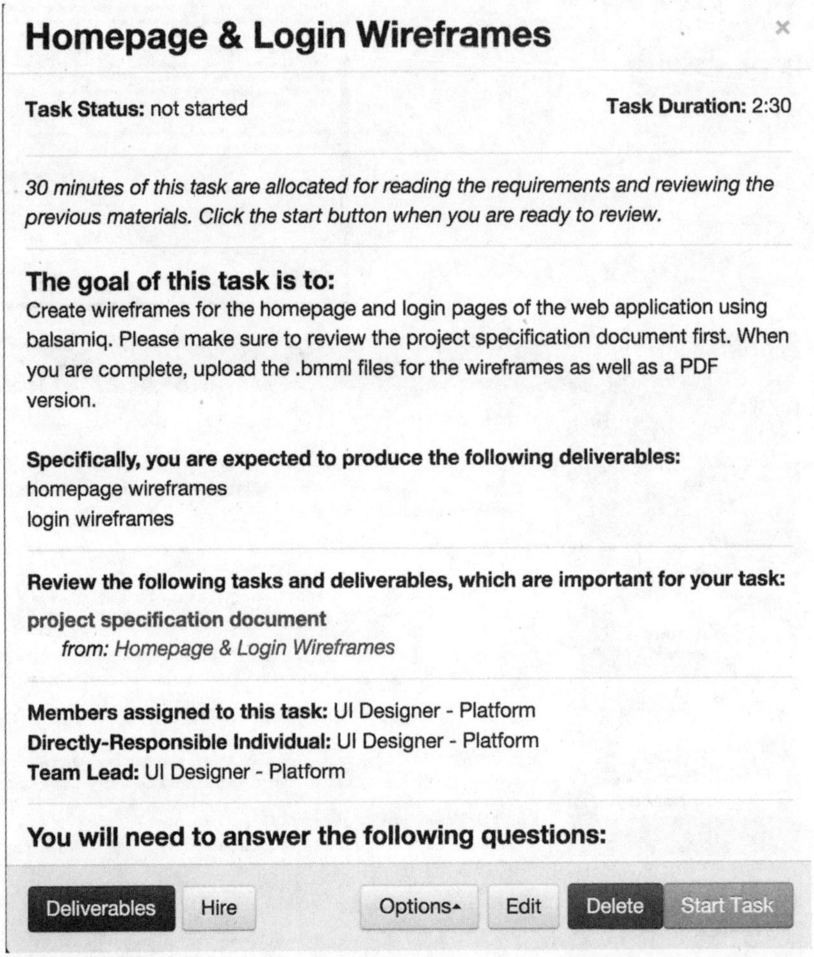

Homepage & Login Wireframes

Task Status: not started **Task Duration:** 2:30

30 minutes of this task are allocated for reading the requirements and reviewing the previous materials. Click the start button when you are ready to review.

The goal of this task is to:
Create wireframes for the homepage and login pages of the web application using balsamiq. Please make sure to review the project specification document first. When you are complete, upload the .bmml files for the wireframes as well as a PDF version.

Specifically, you are expected to produce the following deliverables:
homepage wireframes
login wireframes

Review the following tasks and deliverables, which are important for your task:
project specification document
    from: Homepage & Login Wireframes

Members assigned to this task: UI Designer - Platform
Directly-Responsible Individual: UI Designer - Platform
Team Lead: UI Designer - Platform

You will need to answer the following questions:

[Deliverables] [Hire]   [Options▾] [Edit] [Delete] [Start Task]

Figure 5.3
When workers click on a task block, they get even more details about their work. They see their deadline, their interdependencies, and where to upload their deliverables.

When a worker arrives, their onboarding experience then feels more like a guided lesson than being thrown into the deep end. The software points out to them who they are going to need to coordinate with, where to find those collaborators if the worker needs to talk to them, what the worker's first task is going to be, and what the specific deliverables will be. Of course, in return, the software needs someone—workers or a manager—to add that information to the system.

You can solve these problems without building flash teams software as we have done, or as Gigster built internally. It requires heavy use of templates and over-communication to make sure that workers can be confident that they are doing the right thing.

If you onboard more manually, the film crew thought experiment can help you think it through: the crew arrives but they all need a shared expectation of what the movie is supposed to be like, so that they can make individual decisions in sync with those expectations. They also need information about what their role is expected to do, so that they can jump in and start working autonomously. They do not need all of this explained to them from scratch for each new movie. They rely on a set of tools and artifacts to help them all get on the same page, such as storyboards and shot lists, all acting as a source of shared truth that they can reference to make sure that they are doing the right thing. Without this common understanding of shared vision, shared tools, and respective roles and tasks, a director would need to spend all day micromanaging in order to get things moving.

And that's not a launch—that's a flop.

Set the Stage but Prepare to Change

Creating a flash team is a bit like constructing a lightweight scaffold in the shape of a team—including slots for the specialized roles and for the designated manager—and then rapidly hiring new team members to populate those slots and bring their roles to life. Setting these structures up in advance is key because you are convening teams *on demand* where people will not have worked together before. Yet, even with all that advance planning, you also must be ready to dynamically adapt and change these structures from day one. The complex projects that benefit from on-demand teams involve constantly figuring out the plan as you go and matching the team's efforts to those plans.

Flash teams show that teams can likely be much more dynamic than expected in adapting to new members, new structures, new ideas, and new information. This more adaptive capability is, again, partly about good management and teaming practices and partly about software and tools. The focus on designing the team in advance, for example, invites management practices in which you thoughtfully envision and set up the structures and conditions that people will populate and work in.

This focus reminds us of a provocative statement we heard in graduate school. Richard Hackman, one of the world's experts on teams, would say "Get the conditions right, and the team behaviors will take care of themselves." We take Hackman's comment about getting the conditions right seriously, but with a key addition. Get the conditions right and be ready to adapt those conditions as the situation changes.

Conditions for Role-Based *Teaming*

So: at a bare minimum, get the right roles on scene. And with a little extra design and planning, you can also help the group of roles to cohere as a team. In thinking about designing for teamwork specifically, it's again useful to recognize that many teamwork behaviors are prosocial—done for the good of the group rather than what's good for you. Upon joining a team, people will look at the conditions and will tend to engage in prosocial behaviors only if they see they will be rewarded for doing so.

You *can* do this through team design. This is where you, as the flash team designer, need to create the conditions under which role-based experts arrive on scene and feel jointly responsible for their work in a way that is engaging, fulfilling, and fair. In addition to the more structural designs of flash teams roles and hierarchy, you have the opportunity to design for flash team cohesion. Consider these tactics:

- **Reward Team Performance**: When appropriate, shift from individual task responsibility to team milestones so that members share accountability for their collective performance.
- **Recognize Teaming Behaviors**: Model and celebrate teaming behaviors like sharing information, helping with tasks outside one's role, or actively communicating. Create a culture where members feel motivated to go beyond prescribed roles for team success.

- **Predefine Communication Protocols:** Emphasize and model *closed-loop communication*, a technique frequently used in high-stakes settings like emergency rooms (ERs). Messages are not only sent but confirmed and clarified, creating continuous feedback loops that significantly reduces misunderstandings and errors.
- **Create Shared Workspaces and Tools:** Just as physical layouts like mingled stations in the ER foster teamwork, virtual or physical shared spaces can enhance collaboration. For example, create an online hub with centralized access to tools, resources, and team communication channels where members can see and support each other's work and quickly communicate on the fly.

These tactics help transform flash teams from temporary collections of individuals into cohesive, high-performing teams.

To make these tactics concrete: Valentine studied a team design initiative in hospital ERs and found that something as simple as changing the placement of doctors and nurses in the ER—mingling them into shared stations rather than separating their stations on opposite sides of the department—can result in dramatic improvements in team behaviors and performance.[4] One ER's time to fully treat and discharge a patient dropped 40 percent after the redesign, and staff morale went way up. This was purely a team design success—they had not hired more people and they had not really trained anyone specifically on new skills. They just fixed the conditions in which people were interacting, and the interactions became much more constructive.

When designing a flash team, you'd be looking for how easily people can recognize and communicate with each other as teammates. Have you set up the equivalent of the shared workstation, or do they feel like they're standing across the room from each other, where it is effortful and risky to approach each other and ask questions?

Still, designing for teamwork is challenging—there are many conditions to pay attention to. In our study, other hospital ERs did the same intervention with placing nurses and doctors into little pods together where they could communicate more easily.[5] But in many of those ERs, the small temporary groups still did not develop prosocial teamwork behaviors. Our study showed that the difference was in their sense of collective responsibility or the degree to which they shared accountability for the outcomes of their work.

In the failed ER pods, managers had set up a pooled queue. This meant that a pod would get a new patient only when they were ready for one. Which meant that if some of the team members worked a little slower, they could buffer their team from getting another patient. This perverse incentive that penalized discharging patients basically split the teams. Some team members would drag their feet, and others would work around them to try to get the pods to work.

In the successful ERs where the nurses and doctors in the pods cohered into actively communicating and collaborating teams, they had dedicated queues of patients. That is, no matter how hard you worked, no matter how slowly you treated patients, no matter how difficult the cases were, you were still assigned the next patient who walked through the door if it was your turn. The group was collectively responsible for that growing queue of patients. They had to pull together to be successful. The difference in the teamwork behaviors between these various ERs was remarkable.

We think these are great examples of Olaosebikan's encouragement: "You have to get the launch right." You can design flash teams to be *real teams*, which depends on everyone knowing that they're on a team together—none of this "nurses on one side and doctors on the other side." Everyone on a team needs to access each other for quick easy communication, and they need to feel jointly responsible for their work.[6] This joint responsibility is unusual in the world of online labor markets, where people might be focused only on their individual contracts, wages, or ratings. Here's just one example. Roger Dickey of Gigster told us a funny-not-funny story about a contractor in their network who had figured out how to game the system: he would sign up for a team, get paid for a first milestone, and then bounce. There are plenty of ways that people can be looking out for themselves alone if you don't focus on the team designs that enable true teamwork and collaboration.

6 Adaptation Is a Flash Team Imperative

You've assembled a team of the best and the brightest. They've arrived on scene and, thanks to your carefully planned team design and team launch, they are equipped with an understanding of their roles, the relevant tools, and the project vision. You press "play." What happens next?

Everything changes. Immediately.

The client's initial description is different from what they actually want, the specs weren't communicated clearly and need to be reconfigured, the budget does not accommodate the scope of work being asked for, someone doesn't show up, and as the icing on the cake, someone way overstated their competence at JavaScript. Despite the best-laid plans, a strong team of on-demand experts, and a decent stab at a role structure and a workflow, the overall plan needs to adapt from day one.

Whether you're running a fully remote team as in most of our examples, or a more traditional team, we could all benefit from teams that are more adaptive. But how?

Before we get into the how-to, it's useful to think a little bit more about the design challenge of adaptive teams. We can share some stories on how we learned the hard way to design flash teams that could adapt. We'll start with a thought experiment—what if you just gave *full instructions* to the team members on what *exactly* to do?

Managers Know: Giving Full Instructions Is Hard

"No, Dad! *Open* the jelly!"

A young boy in a viral YouTube clip has written out step-by-step instructions on how to make a peanut butter and jelly sandwich, and his dad is following the instructions with maddening precision.[1] "Get some jelly, rub it on the other half of the bread," the instructions say. So, like a dumb computer program rather than an intelligent adult, the dad grabs the jar of jelly and rubs the unopened jar on the bread. This moment is the premise of the "Exact Instructions Challenge," which illustrates how difficult it is to actually provide instructions on even basic tasks.

Giving instructions is hard because we humans move through the world with so many interpretations of what is going on that we simply take for granted. These interpretations and assumptions are implicit—we do not notice them until we do things like try to articulate specific instructions using language. We take for granted that, *of course*, once you've opened the jelly jar and put a knife into the jar, the next instruction to "put the jelly onto the bread" means to remove a glob of jelly from the jar and put that glob onto the bread. *Of course* you don't set the jelly jar on the bread. A small child already knows to assume that understanding from another human. But that's not what the instructions say. Figuring out how to provide instructions at that level of specificity is difficult—it's not how we think, and it's not how we assume other people think. We assume a level of human understanding from our instructions that can turn pretty good instructions into reasonable actions, given the situation.

How does this relate to adaptive teams? When we have a complex project to complete, we will simply not be able to specify *in advance* a plan that is "good enough" to get the project done. There are two related reasons as to why this is impossible: one, because plans and instructions are hard to specify at the right level of detail; and two, because situations inevitably change. Imagine if you had to explain how to make a peanut butter and jelly sandwich to an alien who knew nothing about sandwiches or silverware. Or you had to account for every possible back-up plan if the peanut butter clumps up or there's no jelly left.

When we start a project, we can use instructions and plans to know how to start, but as situations change—which they inevitably do—we adapt. We do not just blindly keep following the plan (or if we do, that's perhaps a discussion for our therapists rather than our management science professors).

This inevitability of change is a known problem in management. Job descriptions, training manuals, or even best practice sheets are only thin descriptions of what people actually need to do to get a job done. I can hand you a detailed description of my job, and you still wouldn't know exactly what to do to carry out my job. Instructions and plans can be useful resources but can never offer complete instructions for how to actually complete a piece of work.

Workflows Become Irrelevant if They Don't Adapt

When we first started creating flash teams, we were responding to innovations in the research world of crowdsourcing, which was gathering steam in computer science departments around the world. At that time, many researchers—including Bernstein—were demonstrating software workflows that guided "the crowd" on completing complex tasks together. These workflows were like trying to give complete instructions for projects. They tried to anticipate all the work upfront and were impossible to adapt.

We did a proof-of-concept study where we used these predefined workflows to guide teams of experts from Upwork to create software. The experts from Upwork were instructed to follow the software workflows: the user interface designer could hand off the design to the software engineer, who could hand off the prototype to the user experience researcher, and a website was on its way. Or, to create an educational video, an educator and a topic area expert could collaborate on a script, then write a quiz to test for learning mastery afterwards. Simple workflows, complete instructions, crowdsourced experts. In theory, everything was fine.

But in practice, as we tried to run actual flash teams using these workflows and instructions specified in advance, the teams struggled and quickly abandoned the plans. In one case, we provided the expert team with a complex workflow represented as a series of tasks and interdependencies, one flowing to the next. What we liked about that idea, in theory, was that any one team member could join the team, click into the platform, and immediately see what was going on with everyone else and what their first task was. What we saw in practice was that the workflows were out of date almost immediately and then largely abandoned, as team members instead just relied heavily on text chat to adapt and coordinate new plans.[2]

For example, a team member logged on and decided that another programming language was a better fit with the task and his skills. Well, why not? We love a good suggestion! The problem was that in his (possibly quite useful) suggestion, he had started down a whole new workflow with different tasks and interdependencies for his team members. The whole workflow was now defunct. And since the workflow was static and unchangeable, the workflow became unhelpful at best and overly constraining at worst. The team had to work around the obsolete workflow to coordinate and communicate their plans.

Similar complications arose with nearly every flash team. Each team quickly encountered unexpected situations that made the workflows quickly obsolete; they had no structure around how to adapt their collective efforts to a new workflow. Moving on from that point felt inefficient and stressful. Even with lots of prior data and recommended workflows, every flash team will still need to adapt its workflow.

There is no way to specify all of the right actions, no complete set of instructions that can make this all work. And things will change even during the course of work. Again, imagine that your team had to write down a plan at the very beginning of the project and could never deviate from it. At the beginning, things might be fine, and the plan would be a solid guide. But, sooner or later, something unexpected would happen: maybe a slight deviation at the start turns into a bigger change later, or an error throws off the schedule but you're not able to change the plan to account for it. The farther down the path you get, the more changes accumulate and the more the original plan looks like a pipe dream.

We had run into a complexity limit. The activities of working, coordinating, and creating are by nature complex and adaptive. We need to design our teams, our work, and our software with this expectation from the start. Things will change. Immediately. But we can adapt, as a team.

People and Teams *Can* Be Good at Adapting

The good news: unlike instructions or workflows made in advance, people and flash teams *can* be good at adapting. People assigned to expert roles give flash teams (and teams in general) the capabilities that make them good at adapting.

First, let's talk about how people can be good at adapting to changing situations. As human beings, we developed to take in our environment in dynamically ongoing ways. Our sensory processing is fine-tuned to take in a new sound or notice a change in expression on somebody's face or see data on changing weather conditions and know what that means for our

Adaptation Is a Flash Team Imperative

supply chain. The opposite of giving all the instructions up front or specifying all of the right actions that someone should take would be to just let a person figure out what to do based on the situation; to just use human creativity and ingenuity to improvise a situation. Rather than the step-by-step literal instructions, just put a package of bread and jars of peanut butter and jelly on the table and trust that someone could figure it out based on their past experiences with the world.

But we have to be aware of how we also can be bad at adapting, missing changes or interpreting things through biased filters. A fun illustration of this concept is the YouTube video genre called the *attentional challenge*.[3] In one example, you watch someone put a Hershey's Kiss under one of nine cups and try to keep track of where the candy is as the cups are moved and rearranged. What you realize at the end is that you've paid so much attention to where the Hershey's Kiss is that you did not perceive some pretty big basic events in the video—like the moment a duck appears, or a fifth set of hands shows up, or another color of cups gets introduced. Our brains are good at perceiving and interpreting changes in our environment, but they are also good at paying too much attention to some things and interpreting changes based on earlier experiences. You were so caught up in the task at hand that you didn't realize that what the team needed shifted in the meantime.

Second, *groups* of people can also be good at adapting to changing situations. (Again, heavy emphasis on *can be*.) When you have a group, you have many of these adaptive human brains, each of which is a dynamic information processing unit, taking in relevant information from the changing situation. In teams, our information processing can be highly specialized: someone is the look-out while someone else does the heist. Having someone else be lookout means that they are taking in the changing information in the situation that is relevant to getting caught while the other person can focus all of their attention on the task at hand.

In a flash team the division of labor is based on much more specialized expertise. You have very specialized team members who are able to take in relevant information for their role and their position—they can see what in the changing situation is relevant for their own plans. And then, ideally, all of this changing awareness can be combined into a coordinated awareness of the whole situation.

But just as individual human brains have known cognitive biases, groups of human brains have all of those individual biases, plus certain social processes that can get in the way of the group adapting. So, things can go very wrong. A very common example is a team building activity called the hidden profile exercise, in which six people will each have a few pieces of relevant information, and success requires that the team figure out what information needs to be shared between them to realize the hidden connections.[4] The best way to win the exercise is to literally write down everyone's information in a shared document. But somehow the social processes that come up in groups tend to dominate this process and make the group miss sharing some information, discount some other information, and end up making decisions that are poor in hindsight once all information is known.

If the task you're doing is very well understood and routine, you don't need to be quite as vigilant about changes. On the other hand, if the task has a lot of novelty and uncertainty to it, re-planning is inevitable and the team needs to be ready to adapt constantly and continuously. Amy Edmondson of Harvard synthesized this all into what she calls the Process Knowledge Spectrum.[5] For routine, predictable tasks, teams can rely more on instructions, checklists, and standard operating procedures with minimal adaptation. However, as tasks become less routine—requiring judgment, creativity, or responsiveness to rapidly changing conditions—teams need to engage in continuous monitoring, reassessment, and communication. This adaptability is especially essential in tasks where new information can arise at any moment, demanding immediate updates to the plan. Flash teams, built for dynamic coordination, are particularly suited to operating on the adaptive end of this spectrum, where real-time problem solving and agility are critical.

In sum, the human team is a powerful coordination tool. Human minds are good at adapting to new information in context and coming up with new ideas about what to do. Humans are good at improvising. If humans are good at improvising, then groups of humans can also be good at improvising and adapting. But it does require the group members to actively read a situation and update their mental models about what is happening and communicate it well to group members, and for group members to take in the new information from each other and make a new plan. That's true of any team, and flash teams have the added benefit of being enabled by some software tools that can help with coordination.

Adaptation Is a Flash Team Imperative

Next, we'll show more about how software can help flash teams become dynamically adaptive. The opposite fail mode to pre-specified plans and rigid workflows is an overreliance on constant communication on chat because there is no relevant structure or plan, and where people inevitably miss what's changing and what's going on. And of course, nobody really wants to be the one keeping the team documentation up to date because the workflow is in continual flux. How do we keep teams adaptive without requiring them to document every single step they are taking? We'll dig into that approach in the next chapter.

7 Enabling Flash Team Adaptation through Software

Sabina, excited to join a new flash team, clicked into her first task. Her heart sank. She had been assigned a user experience (UX) task, but she was an expert in creating user interfaces (UI) screens and was ready to work on the team's UI design.

Somehow, her new manager, Brooke, had hired her as a UI designer but had assigned her work that veered into the realm of UX research—something Sabina wasn't equipped to handle. Instead of sketching out user interfaces, she found herself tasked with figuring out how existing screen elements would integrate with the front-end developers' code—a UX-heavy responsibility she hadn't anticipated.

Sabina quickly messaged Brooke. Together, they acknowledged the common confusion that arises between UI and UX tasks, and that Sabina had clearly been caught in that ambiguity. Brooke immediately saw the mismatch. Sabina's skills were still valuable, but not in the role originally assigned.

Brooke went to the flash team dashboard, which displayed the shared workflow the entire team was following. She created a new branch off the current tasks and added a new box—"Design UI screens"—that she assigned specifically to Sabina. In the public Slack channel, she posted a message clarifying the role shift: "Sabina is going to help with UI screens now."

Within an hour of joining the team, Sabina's role had been reconfigured and she started her first design task. The process had been seamless—her manager had restructured the workflow in real time, ensuring both the project and her contributions stayed aligned. This fluid adjustment reflected the team's ability to adapt to shifting needs while keeping the workflow visible to everyone, ensuring clarity and collaboration.

So far, we have shown that, to create a flash team, you first design the right role structure and populate it through smart, automated, on-demand hiring. You take certain steps to get the launch right, and you design the conditions for teamwork in advance. And, based on the last chapter, you are ready and expecting to adapt all your planning, designing, and hiring from day one. This chapter tells you how we enable on-demand, remote teams of experts to effectively read changing situations and adapt on the fly.

Flash teams teach us that we can design rapid adaptation directly into our management strategies and software tools. In this chapter, we'll introduce a strategy to empower teams to adapt effectively, constantly, and on the fly. The big idea is to create a shared (smart) image of the team's organizational chart with the related role structure and task timeline. And, most importantly, then empower *everyone* on the team to dynamically edit the image to propose changes to the roles, role structures, hierarchies, tasks, and timeline. As those edits come in, the whole group maintains an up-to-date image of the flash team, even as it changes.

In the earlier chapters, we shared examples from adaptive temporary organizations such as ERs and film crews. Dynamic temporary teams adapt based on their clearly defined roles, which evolve based on the situation needs rather than on knowing each other well. And when the situation is complex enough to demand "teams of teams," they similarly rely on dynamic hierarchy in the form of sets of managers who help coordinate the complexity of the work (more on that in chapter 8). When we say *hierarchy*, we mean an organizational structure where a manager has more decision-making power and accountability for overseeing and directing the actions of team members.

For example, imagine a global company facing a cybersecurity breach that impacts multiple markets. A crisis management team is immediately assembled, pulling in specialists from cybersecurity, IT, legal, communications, and compliance, all from different offices and time zones. Many of these team members have never worked together before, and their organizational affiliations vary. Despite the lack of familiarity, the team rapidly organizes itself around their specialized roles. The cybersecurity lead manages the technical investigation. The legal team oversees regulatory compliance, while communications crafts messaging for key stakeholders. The group then adapts as needed. For example, if a particular legal requirement arises in one region, the legal lead delegates specific tasks to the regional expert. Similarly, the cybersecurity lead adjusts assignments based on the evolving technical issues, such as patching vulnerabilities or negotiating with attackers.

The role structure and hierarchy need to be adaptable, and the main point of this chapter is that software can help. When we were designing the flash teams software, we were led by this question: how could software enable complex groups of experts to adapt to changing conditions on the fly?

Role-Based Software Helps Flash Teams Adapt

We knew the foundation had to be in enabling the role structures and hierarchies to become adaptive. We looked to software design that encoded those foundational design principles. Temporary teams swarm around a new project and immediately begin to contribute their expertise. Film crews and disaster response teams can adapt quickly because they're not focused on a workflow—they are focused on adapting their *roles*.

Like these temporary organizations, software for adaptive flash teams must be organized around *roles, not workflows*. Tasks and workflows can be present, to be sure, but they cannot be the focus. Instead, the software needs to allow every person who lands into the group to know immediately what their role is; how it relates to others' roles in the organization; how to communicate; and how to coordinate. In short, we need to support the exact same kinds of common-sense decisions that people in temporary organizations perform. The platform needs to visualize my role, my manager's role, where to work, how to talk to others. How do we enable software to support the dynamism and adaptation at which temporary organizations excel, without their face-to-face interaction, shared physical environment, and fast-paced verbal communication?

Foundry, the software that we developed for flash teams, starts with a role orientation: when we hire online workers, our software hires by the role title ("Animation inbetweener") and makes clear where the role fits in the overall role hierarchy ("You report to the Animation Director").[1]

We can't just ask teams to keep a platform up to date to adapt those roles or the hierarchy, because nobody will. (When was the last time that you went and excitedly filled out documentation for a project you're working on?) The work process needs to align incentives—any information that people need must be produced as a byproduct of their work. We also can't restrict the flash team to having just one person able to edit it at a time. Imagine the bottleneck that would result if the engineering team needed to adjust their deliverables at the same time as the quality assurance lead is changing dependencies. In any nontrivially sized organization, multiple things are likely to evolve at once. But if anyone could edit the source code at any time, like in a shared Google Doc, chaos could erupt and you'd have less coordination, not more.

So, what do we do?

Empower the Team to Edit the Team's "Source Code"

Think of the roles, hierarchy, tasks, and workflows of the flash team as the *source code* of the flash team: the team's raw DNA. In computing, source code is the computer code that defines a program—it's not the user interface that you see, but the underlying algorithms that are running. When a flash team, like a fire crew, needs to adapt, it needs to change its own source code. What we need to do is empower team members to edit that source code—the roles, hierarchy, tasks, and workflows—as they work and broadcast the change out to the entire group. If you need a new team member, or you need more time on a task, or you want to propose that a team pause and rework a part of the strategy, you're changing the source code of the flash team.

If you think of the flash team as being defined by that source code, then we can draw on a metaphor from software development to help flash teams adapt. In software development, a best practice involves using something called *version control* to keep source code in sync, even across gigantic codebases. You may have heard of tools like Git, or its popular hosted version called GitHub.[2] Despite many moving parts in software, version control helps keep things in sync.

Here are the steps of version control on platforms like GitHub. We describe them in detail here because this is the mental model of how we can make flash teams software adaptable and editable for anyone on the team. Traditional modern version control takes place in five steps:

1. Branch: create a copy of the current codebase, called a *branch* of that codebase, that you can edit without changing what other people see.
2. Edit: change the source code on your branch, proposing any edits that you think ought to be made. Since you have your own branch, your edits don't mess up anybody else's work.

Enabling Flash Team Adaptation through Software   67

3. Pull request: make a formal request to someone above you in the hierarchy to review the changes that you've made in your branch.
4. Review: the person who reviews the pull request can see exactly what changes you are proposing to merge into the main branch, leave comments, iterate, and eventually approve it.
5. Merge: the approved changes from your branch are applied back to the main branch, working out any conflicting changes that got merged in by others in the meantime.

Inspired by this branch-and-merge method for keeping a complex shared artifact in sync, even as everyone makes changes, we designed flash teams to be able to follow the same process.

Recall we are thinking of their roles, hierarchies, tasks, and workflows as the teams' own source code. With this model, we could allow any member in the team to edit any of those elements. They would similarly branch the flash team's structures and propose changes to any of those structures in their own private branch. Then, their branch could be automatically compared to the structures in the current flash team, with the software visually highlighting the differences being proposed.

In software engineering land, this process is called making a *pull request* on source code. You're asking the main branch to "pull in" your changes. Whenever someone edits the flash team and submits their proposal, someone has to approve it. We configured our flash teams so that the proposal travelled up the hierarchy for approval: for example, a manager needs to approve the changes, their manager needs to approve any changes that they propose, and so on. And then when the pull request was approved, the software automatically announces the change and updates everybody's interfaces and information.

Once the change gets approved, the flash team software immediately acts on it.

- Did the change add a new role? Then the software immediately kicks off the hiring process and puts out a call to the labor market to hire.
- Did the change impact deliverables or hierarchy? The software updates any members whose roles need to know about the change.

Connecting the action to the pull request also better solves the incentive problem of encouraging people to actually use the software: if they want to let their manager know they need more time, or need additional help, the

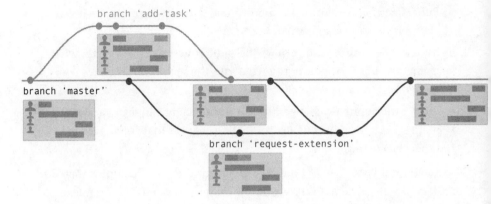

Figure 7.1
Foundry encoded adaptable role structures and hierarchy via a pull request system. Any team member could edit any of the roles, hierarchy, workflows, or tasks, which would create a private branch. Then, their branch could be automatically compared to the structures in the current flash team, with the software visually highlighting the differences being proposed.

pull request is how they do it. This approach allows both top-down organizational changes as well as bottom-up changes driven by team members.

Software Enables Change through "Pull Requests"

There is real power to using software to support adaptive teaming, as opposed to winging it using Slack or other unstructured communication tools. Some of that power comes from the dynamic user interface. It can offer a dashboard that is customized by role. In fact, if you just sign up for a project management software like Asana, you might notice that you first tell it the role you're acting in, and then the whole dashboard is customized to support you in that role.

It's the same idea for flash teams software: all of the structures and conditions that we were describing above can be visualized in personalized ways. It can communicate your role, the overall role structure, your manager's role, and the overall organizational structure. All of that can be edited to respond to changing conditions. The UI can also encode helpful conditions—like who is online and available, where to find each other for fast-paced communication, who is responsible for different tasks, and what the status is.

To understand why pull request-style adaptation of flash teams is so important, we're going to return to the story of the UI team that kicked off the chapter. We do this to give you a real sense of what it's like to be part of a rapidly adapting flash team.

When we last left Sabina, she had realized that her manager had assigned her UX tasks that she did not know how to do. Sabina's manager Brooke now needed to pivot the team to accommodate Sabina's unexpected constraint and to hire a front-end developer who could do the tasks that required skills and experience that Sabina lacked. Brooke created a branch, drew a new task box—"Design UI screens"—and assigned it to Sabina. The pull request got merged, but again something went wrong: when Sabina saw her new revised work plan, she was happy to see that most of it was reasonable and within her skill set, but was equally concerned that she was going to need more hours to complete the task than Brooke had allotted. So, this time Sabina was the one who created a pull request: in her branch, she proposed additional time. Within a few minutes, she saw that Brooke had approved that pull request, so that the workflow now reflected her task box with more time to do her work.

In the meantime, Sabina's manager Brooke still needed the UX development work done. She made a separate pull request that added a task for UX development, but since there was no one on the team who could do it, the platform needed to send out a message to everyone in the UI/UX development pool to hire a new team member.

The platform sent out a message, and within 25 minutes, Martin from Slovenia had accepted the job and joined the team. Martin quickly got up to speed and started completing tasks. He finished the first one Brooke had envisioned, and after chatting actively with the team in the Slack channel, recognized where he could be helpful next. Now the changes came from the bottom up: Martin created a new branch and drew a new task box for himself, suggesting the next task he could do and the relevant parameters as to how long it would take, when his proposed deadline was, and so on. His suggested task appeared in a pull request for Brooke on her screen over in Egypt, and as the manager, she approved the pull request. That approval pushed the change to everyone else's interface, and Martin got to work.

Sabina and Brooke and Martin were all using our flash teams software to adapt on the fly and to keep in sync with each other as the situation changed. Behind the scenes, what the software was doing was classic version control, along the lines of how GitHub works for software developers. The flash team software was keeping a *main* version of this team's workflow and role structure, and keeping that main branch consistent for everyone across their various screens. When Sabina wanted to make a change, she just started editing the workflow on her screen. The software took her edits as a copy of the flash team workflow and kept it as a copy until Brooke had a chance to review the proposed edits as a pull request. When Brooke approved the pull request, the software then pushed the new version of the workflow out to everyone's else's screen.

We achieve all of this for our flash teams using the custom Foundry software that we developed. It will not surprise us in the least if project management software for flash teams starts enabling similar functionality in the next few years. But, what should you do in the meantime?

The first step to enabling adaptation in your own flash teams is to make sure that there is some sort of shared visibility of the team's source code. The roles, tasks, and hierarchy could exist in project management software like Asana or GitHub Projects, or they might just be listed in a shared Google Sheet that is visible to everyone on the team. Then, you need some way for people to propose changes to it. Our software follows a fairly structured flow for changes—you propose, your manager approves, the software integrates it and notifies everyone—but your team can do this manually without software support. For example, tell your team, "Before you make any changes to the plan on this page, get your manager's approval." This is a bit more heavyweight than what we built, and there's the possibility of miscommunication if what the worker thought they were proposing is not what the manager thought they were approving, but it will work in a pinch.

So, while software makes adaptation much smoother, keeps records, and otherwise makes life better, you absolutely can adapt your flash teams without custom software in the meantime.

Examples of Adapting On-the-Fly with Flash Teams

Across a series of flash teams that we've now run, adaptation is nearly universal. How universal? We set out to measure it. We recruited three flash team "CEOs"—people who had a meaningful project that they wanted done—and we gave them each our flash team software, a budget, and a deadline of six weeks to achieve their goals. The teams whose work we measured were these:

- The EMS Trauma Report Team: We talked about Mark in the introduction to this book. Mark is an emergency room doctor who envisioned mobile tablet software that would alert the ER to trauma cases ahead of their arrival at the hospital.
- The True Story Gaming Team: This set of podcasters wanted to create and playtest a card game version of their podcast.
- The Enterprise Workshop Planning Portal: This team at Accenture that wanted to create a custom enterprise-branded software portal for organizing internal workshops. This is the same Accenture team that we described at the beginning of chapter 4.

Each of these teams started with nobody except the CEO and our flash teams software. In the six weeks that these teams had to achieve their goal, they adapted constantly. The most instructive measurement is changes per day—the median number of merged pull requests each day. These organizations had a median of *four changes per day*. That worked out to hundreds of adaptations—over three hundred of them, in the case of EMS Trauma Report—where these teams were reconfiguring themselves over the six weeks.

Adaptations came from all over the team hierarchy. The majority—68 percent—came from middle management, as leads of subteams updated tasks, roles, and hiring. Twenty-two percent of them were bottom-up from workers on the front lines of the project. And the remainder, a bit under 10 percent, came from the CEOs of the flash teams themselves, as they set new strategic directions or changed the overall hierarchy.

What were these adaptations doing? The teams used our flash teams software to add people, tasks, teams, and time, and revise groupings, hierarchy, and task requirements. Here are some examples:

Bottom-Up Adaptations

Teams often implemented changes initiated by team members themselves, showcasing organic adjustments to task focus and workflow:

- Example 1: In the EMS Trauma Report team, a marketer recognized that a task focused on creating a hiring page could be more effectively directed at promoting app features. With team support, they coordinated four pull requests to adjust the page content.

EMS Trauma Report — Android Application & Website

True Story — Card Game, Android Application & Website

Enterprise Workshop Planning Portal — Web Application

Figure 7.2
Flash teams successfully produced complex deliverables, including mobile tablet software for emergency responders to send advance information to hospitals, a card game version of a podcast, and a custom software portal for organizing internal workshops. Each project started with only the CEO and the flash teams software but each integrated many changes and thirty or more team members during the project.

- Example 2: The software QA team in the Enterprise Workshop Portal proactively created pull requests to add tasks for quality testing, ensuring each new feature from the software engineers would meet standards, adapting as the engineering team's pace evolved.

Top-Down Directives

CEOs or senior leaders introduced structural changes or created new roles to guide and unify project direction

- Example 1: True Story CEOs realized that the poems created for their game cards needed a cohesive style, prompting them to establish a Chief Poetry Officer role.
- Example 2: In EMS Trauma Report, the CEO recognized exceptional performance by a backend engineer, resulting in a new leadership role through a formal pull request.

Large-Scale Overhauls and Task Reconfigurations

Some adaptations significantly expanded project scope or redefined team structures and task allocations:

- Example 1: True Story decided just a week before their deadline to add a mobile app to complement their card game. To execute this complex pivot, they hired an Android app manager who formed a new team, driving over 50 pull requests in a rapid push to completion.
- Example 2: The Enterprise Workshop Portal's CEO continuously reshaped the hierarchy by shifting roles and scope in response to team needs and external feedback, enabling dynamic project adjustments.

New Strategic Directions and Compliance

New requirements and regulatory needs sometimes led to unexpected organizational changes:

- Example 1: The EMS Trauma Report team found that HIPAA compliance was necessary for storing medical data. The CEO resourcefully hired a web security engineer from Egypt and worked with a university compliance officer to lay the groundwork for data security.
- Example 2: Stakeholder feedback prompted the EMS Trauma Report team to spin up user research and marketing roles, adapting the app's features based on rigorous testing and market research.

Of course, some changes happened outside the software too, and that's entirely all right. Imagine needing to make a pull request for every small tweak. These small tweaks, like minor bug fixes, don't really require new resources or information broadcast to the larger group for awareness, so the teams just got it done in those cases. We suspect that integrating with project planning software or issue tracking software might help ease the burden and keep everything more in sync.

In some cases, we heard feedback from workers that the ability to adapt was almost *too* powerful. Have you ever worked with a manager who can't look ahead more than a few days at a time? Workers occasionally complained to us that the CEOs made such heavy use of the adaptation framework that it felt like they didn't really have a solid plan at the beginning. That makes sense: we will always need to adapt, but minimizing the amount of unnecessary adaptation will likely be appreciated by the team. We'll talk about the role of leaders in all this next.

8 Mobilizing Hierarchy for Dynamic Adaptation

Imagine two teams, Alpha and Bravo, tasked with building a new app feature for a high-profile client.[1] Both teams have top talent—experienced developers, creative designers, and seasoned project managers. And both teams have plenty of unexpected things that start to go wrong. Yet, Team Alpha delights the client and comes in on time and on budget, and Team Bravo does not. What's the difference?

Team Alpha is prepared to adapt from the start. Their project manager, Elena, establishes clear communication channels on day one. She sets up a shared project board and Slack channel for everyone to track progress and ensures that all discussions happen in public threads. From the outset, Elena insists on transparency. Handoffs between designers and developers are well-coordinated. When the front-end team finishes a design, it is immediately posted with detailed documentation, and the back-end developers know exactly when to pick it up.

When a sudden change in client requirements comes through, Team Alpha doesn't panic. Elena quickly organizes a meeting, pulling in the relevant specialists. She listens to the concerns of the designers who feel the change may affect the user experience and also the developers who anticipate technical challenges. She balances these perspectives, clarifies the new priorities, and makes sure the team adjusts roles and timelines accordingly. Everyone on the team knows their next step and who to ask if there are further questions.

In contrast, Team Bravo's manager assumed that people were more in sync than they were. She did not notice that from the start, there was confusion over roles. Communication is sporadic, often happening in private messages or scattered emails. Deadlines are missed, bugs aren't fixed in time, and the client is frustrated by the limited updates. Team Bravo's project manager, though capable, is missing how much everyone is missing each other and doesn't intervene to synchronize efforts or clarify expectations. Handoffs between team members are messy and unclear, with incomplete information passed along. By the end of the project, the feature is delivered late, and it fails to meet client expectations, and the company takes a reputation hit with the client.

The key difference in these team outcomes is the project managers' leadership. Elena actively managed the flow of information, ensuring single-source-of-truth (SSOT) documentation and seamless handoffs. She was always thinking ahead and anticipating the unanticipated conflicts and integration issues that inevitably arose. Her consistent oversight, combined with her skill in adapting the team's focus to the client's shifting needs, was the glue that held her team together.

In the previous chapter, we focused on how flash teams can become dynamically adaptive by leveraging the dynamism of role structures and some truly adaptive software practices. In so doing, we temporarily set aside the role of managers and hierarchy in producing dynamically adapting teams. But that's what this chapter is all about.

Hierarchy refers to a team or organizational structure where decision-making power and accountability are distributed across different levels, with higher levels typically overseeing and directing the actions of lower levels. In practical terms, hierarchy offers a framework for managing complex tasks by clarifying who is responsible for what, how information flows, and who has decision rights.

We get that "managers" and "hierarchy" may not be the first word associations that come up when you hear "dynamic" or "adapt." That's okay. We can start with a few inspiring visions. One of our favorite movies growing up—we were teenagers in the 1990s—was *The Fugitive*.[2] In that movie, a funny and sarcastic Tommy Lee Jones leads a team of US Marshals on a chase through forests, tunnels, dams, and much of Chicago to find the fugitive played by Harrison Ford. Jones is the intrepid manager dynamically adapting to the changing situation. He deploys his team members where needed and pulls in new teams and resources immediately as the situation requires.

A great example is a scene in which Harrison Ford leaps from a dam. In the scene, Ford has driven a stolen ambulance into a tunnel. Cops in cars are on one side, and a helicopter has landed on the other side. He's trapped. There's no way out. Jones and team get out of the helicopter and start to converge in the middle of the tunnel.

The situation changes: Ford is nowhere to be found—he's crawled into the pipes in the tunnel. It's no longer a "converge on the fugitive in the tunnel" situation. We're now in a "chase through the pipes" situation: Jones reconfigures his approach and leads his team down into the pipes. By the end of the scene, he has Ford at gunpoint at the end of a pipe that opens out into a huge waterfall over a dam.

Harrison Ford starts to kneel down, captured. Then he leaps from the dam. Jones is astonished. The situation has changed yet again. He's now in a "fugitive in the river below" situation. His immediate pivot is a master class in dynamically adapting to a changing situation. He shouts:

We need helicopters, divers . . .
 Turn that water off . . .
 Put two patrol cars on that bridge . . .
 Put four patrols up there and have them canvas that river upstream and down . . .
 I want to see a helicopter a hundred feet up from this river . . . make them aware of these wires . . .
 I want hounds on both banks upstream and downstream . . .
 [*to the locals*] Do you have a search and rescue team? Get them down here sweeping that riverbed . . .[3]

That's how quickly he understands that he's in a new situation, and how quickly he spins up his own team and countless other teams to respond to the changing situation. We'll let you watch the movie for the rest of it. (Spoiler: the fugitive doesn't die, isn't actually guilty, and serves up Jones and team many more changing situations, which they adapt to like champs. It's a fun classic!)

When *New York Times* reporter Noam Scheiber covered our flash teams work, he focused a lot on the key role of team managers in facilitating flash teams working well. We hadn't seen it as clearly until he wrote his article. He predicted, "Yet the flash model appears to have revolutionary potential. If nothing else, millions of middle-management jobs that fell by the wayside in recent decades might one day be reincarnated as freelance project-manager positions."[4] In this chapter, we can spell out with examples why we agree with his prediction.

We'll focus on two main functions for managers in coordinating dynamically adaptive teams. First, managers do some work of coordination: the flash teams equivalent of the Tommy Lee Jones scene. And second, managers relationships to other managers can be a social network that gets activated to accomplish more complex changes. We'll talk about that in chapter 9.

An Integrating View: Managers' Birdseye Role in Coordination

Hierarchy plays an often-undervalued role in coordination having to do with different people's vantage points, or what they can see and pay attention to. When people are carrying out their individualized and specialized roles, they have to pay attention to the details of the task right in front of them: counting chest compressions, for example, while carefully monitoring how much pressure they are putting on the patient's chest. Or securing the airway. Both of these specialized tasks can be all-consuming to get right, and neither of those specialized experts have the attention available to notice that the patient is still on the gurney and needs to be moved to the bed for the next care steps to happen. Instead, the person who is in charge of—is in the hierarchical position to—run the overall patient response can take in the whole scene and help shout out instructions that keep the whole group in sync.

Similarly, across the whole ER, each set of nurses needs to focus on the set of patients in front of them. But the charge nurse, who is running the flow of the whole ER, has the vantage point of what's happening across every single section or pod within the ER and can send additional resources where they're needed if someone gets backed up, or can call in for diagnostics on why there's a backup. Organizational hierarchy offers the template for how information flows in a group, who has decision rights and accountability for different decisions, and a map for how interdependent groups need to coordinate their efforts: for example, making sure that your website's front-end developers are regularly syncing with your back-end developers.

These key functions are why project managers (PMs) can really make or break a team. Katharina Lix of Stanford University did an in-depth study of project managers and freelance teams working at Gigster.[5] One of the engineers she interviewed said, "The PM makes or breaks the team. You can have the best engineers in the world, but if there's not a PM who acts as the glue and makes sure everything runs smoothly and who keeps the client happy, there's no guarantee anything will work."[6] Another told her, "If the PM does a bad job, you get anarchy."[7] The project managers that she talked to explained that they had to adapt their management strategies and processes to the backgrounds of and relationships between the members of each team. Lix noted that managers considered it "challenging and fun to make sure that the client's experience was as smooth and consistent as possible."[8] They enjoyed managing "highly diverse and dynamic teams 'behind the scenes'" and "successfully translating information back and forth" between clients and teams.[9]

With the well-known concerns about hierarchy, let's talk about why a set of managers can be more useful than well-designed roles and workflows at coordinating groups through a complex task. Why aren't the role structures enough? Doesn't everyone know what to do now, by virtue of their roles?

Managers Own Everything Outside the Plan (Which Is So Many Things)

Managers end up owning all of the complexity that is not easily folded into each person's job. It would seem that well-defined, specialized roles should be expansive and adaptive enough to take in unexpected tasks. But that turns out to be as unrealistic as the idea that it is possible to write instructions for even simple tasks. In practice, it is very difficult to anticipate all of the complexity that comes up once a team starts working together.

Managers end up responsible for all of what management professors call *residual complexity*: the inevitable daily contingencies of work. These would include someone not showing up for their job. Or resolving goal conflict between roles: the designer wants to spend more money on design, the developer wants to spend more money on development. That gets escalated to a manager, who is responsible for breaking the tie on the conflict. Or interpersonal conflict develops: someone took credit for someone else's work and they need help resolving the issue. Or some random decision that comes up that no one thought to anticipate and assign to someone—like signing up and registering across all social media accounts. When you hired a social media marketer, they expected to create content but not manage the accounts—who fills in the gap? Likely a manager.

This idea of managers being responsible for residual complexity has been investigated in several research studies.[10] For example, one study looked at the way that different companies set up their relationships with each other—such as exploring the nature of their contracts with each other.[11] The study found that the more complex the relationship between the two entities, the more likely they were to structure a hierarchical entity to govern their relationship—they didn't trust a simple contract to be able to govern all the complexity. They needed a human manager or governance body to deal with all of the complexity they could not anticipate.

We saw this over and over in our flash teams experiments, where we ended up needing an integrating, coordinating managerial role. We discussed in an earlier chapter that one of our flash organizations created a card game that had a deck of cards, each with a poem on it. We discussed how we hired a dozen or so people from Upwork to write poetry for this card game, and how the CEOs noticed that the tone and style of the poems were not as coherent as they would have liked. This turned out to be a job for hierarchy. Hierarchy isn't always just about power dynamics and fiat—it can also simply be about integrating across many disparate parts into a coherent whole. The resulting "Chief Poetry Officer" had the style of poem that the CEOs liked the best, so they asked her to manage the many interesting creative poems and create a coherent style across the many poems. This story is a great example of treating hierarchy more flexibly and dynamically. The poetry team didn't last forever, and the Chief Poetry Officer was in that helpful role for maybe a day. The hierarchical role was more about what needed to be done than about anyone being in charge of anyone else in a lasting way.

Skillful Managers Help Their Teams Be Adaptive

Based on our research, we can also get practical and specific about what effective managers do in their daily work to help coordinate dynamically adaptive teams. They help define the goals and scope of work, often by talking with the client. And they help manage the choreography of information and resources.

Translating Client Vision into a Team Design

Managers are essential for clarifying the clients' goals and expectations. In our studies, once someone understood they were the manager of the team, they immediately started asking questions to help the clients articulate what they wanted done. It reminded us a bit of general contractors, who tend to really know their stuff, including how to help all of the relevant specialists integrate their plans and work seamlessly. Our clients did not generally have experience managing technical projects; they had visions of what they wanted to create. At the start of each of these projects, the team of managers asked questions to help those clients better communicate what they wanted to build. They then did the essential work of translating the clients' visions into role structures, actual tasks and workflows for their teams. Watching the team of managers map the clients' ambiguous visions onto the specific work of their teams was impressive. These flash teams were only as successful as these managers were effective at translating the client's vision into specific team deliverables—and coordinating among themselves how their teams would work together.

We met the CEO of a company that helps staff temporary teams of experts for their clients. Niti Agrawal, CEO of Stage 4 Solutions, told us that this process of defining the statement of work (SOW) is one of the most important keys to a project's success. A manager that can do a good job defining a SOW is going to have a more successful team. She remembered one of her team managers doing this well: the client was a marketing leader at a Fortune 500 Software As A Service (SaaS) provider. They needed help building a new strategy and execution plan for a developer conference. Two of Agrawal's experts first assessed the developers' needs and then developed clear objectives for the conference. As they worked to develop the SOW, they realized that the focus of the conference must be on developer education and hands-on training. They crafted a conference agenda focused on this goal and ensured that marketing materials included the learning attendees would gain. This approach led to a successful event in terms of attendance and post-event survey results and led to a new model for developer events. Had the manager not realized that education and training were the underlying needs of the client, the conference would have been an unfocused failure.

Managers tend to be good at eliciting requirements for a good SOW when they think of this as an exercise in communication. These kinds of activities involve reading documentation, interviewing stakeholders, facilitating meetings, prototyping, observing. Success means communicating to arrive at clarity in what the client wants, even when the clients are not fully clear on it themselves at any moment. It also includes communicating that newfound clarity clearly in instructions and visuals that help team members know what to do.

Orchestrating the Flow of Information and Resources

Managers affect their teams' success in how they help orchestrate various resources such as role clarity and information. Lix had a front-row seat watching the work of hundreds of flash teams at Gigster. For the final study in her dissertation, she pored over the entire written record of six different flash teams, three that had finished their projects and gotten top client feedback and three that had not.[12] As she read and re-read the Slack transcripts and project documentation, she discovered that the project managers of the successful projects acted very differently from the project managers in the teams that had struggled.

The leaders of the successful teams had enabled those teams to develop role clarity and a collective resilience to adapt to problems. One interesting theme was how actively and deftly the project managers managed information specifically to ensure the group outcomes. They consistently brought conversations into the public channels, they established communication protocols and channels, they established central repositories, they ensured there was a single source of truth about goals and processes, and they brought specific experts' attention to relevant information in public channels.

As an example, two engineers engaged in a long multi-hour debugging session in a public Slack channel, just as the team had agreed on. At the end of their conversation, the team leader, who had not been actively involved in the conversation but who had tracked it enough to understand the implications of the changes for the team, tagged a designer on Slack with his relevant to-dos, which the designer subsequently confirmed in a response on Slack.[13] In these teams with managers who engaged in the active information curation practices, there was no evidence of teams having trouble locating the information they needed. Recall these are fully remote and temporary flash teams whose members have never met before. But their managers promoted a clear information environment with single-source-of-truth (SSOT) documentation. They also constantly promoted public transparent conversations and posting.

The project managers on the successful teams also helped ensure the success of handoffs between one team member and the next, whereas the managers on less successful teams did not take an active role in helping with handoffs. Two elements determined the success of handoffs. First, the timing of the handoff mattered. Initiating the handoff too early (i.e., before one team member's output was ready to be passed on for further processing) or too late usually caused delays. Second, the effectiveness of the handoff mattered, specifically whether the handoff involved effective exchange of information that resulted in shared understanding among team members about who needed to do what next. These decisions were mostly owned by the team members, but active managers also took responsibility for ensuring the timing and effectiveness of the handoffs.

This quote snippet illustrates a small moment of team leadership: "@ Engineer when you get a moment today, could you coordinate with @ Designer on the Sparkle aspects of the design for the app/ video? Here (link) is the latest [mockup] from @Designer of the app."[14] With this clear and specific message, the designer and engineer began coordinating immediately, and the team leader had ensured that there was no confusion around which version of the designs they needed to coordinate.

Finally, throughout all of this coordination work, the project managers helped scaffold the sense of role clarity and specialization on the team, even as everyone coordinated actively. Their information management work helped with this role clarity, especially as they assigned tasks in the public Slack channels at the beginning of each milestone and tagged directly responsible individuals for every task. The visibility of responsibilities among team members led to a shared understanding of each other's specializations and expertise. This awareness helped members know whom to approach with questions on specific topics. Additionally, the team members, now aware of each other's expertise (despite working together for the first time), proactively tagged each other as they shared relevant information on Slack, ensuring nothing was overlooked.

9 Mobilizing Hierarchy as a Network for Change

The project was in serious danger of failing—the flash team's technical leadership was not delivering, and they had made several iffy decisions. Then Steve, one of the front-line software engineers, staged a successful management coup to rescue the project. He took over the most powerful management position on the flash team he had joined, and together with his close collaborators on the engineering team, oversaw all of the functions and delivered a successful project.

To rescue the project and take over management of the flash team, Steve convinced the client to approve a major change in technical framework after more than a week had passed in the four-week project. That change was not strictly necessary—the team could have completed the project using either approach. But he was an expert in the new framework, whereas several of the original managers were not.

This change meant the original managers no longer had the relevant expertise to manage a front-end or back-end team in this particular development project and they became obsolete almost overnight. So Steve and his main team collaborators became the leads for the whole flash organization. They worked closely with the client to deliver a successful project within the short time they had left.

Good news for the new leadership team and the client, but a frustrating experience for the original managers. What happened? As the study sponsors, we were somewhat aware that something like this was happening in real time, but it was only after the study when we were analyzing all of the data that we really understood what had gone down. We'll share the story because it illustrates our next point: that the *network* of managers in a flash team can be a powerful structure for accomplishing dynamic adaptation and change.

The Power of a Linking Pin Position in a Network

When we analyzed the full set of Slack messages for these projects, we saw that many of the team members went around their managers and approached the clients directly with ideas or complaints, but the clients consistently routed them back to their managers. Why in this case was the direct pitch to change the entire technical framework to the client successful? What was distinctive about Steve was that he had created what management experts call a *linking pin position*: he had strong ties to his own team members, he had strong upward ties with the client, and he ended up with strong lateral ties to managers of other teams.

He developed these ties by simply stepping in whenever someone needed help planning, doing, or repairing some piece of work. If someone asked a question, he would direct message (DM) them with ideas and help. He became indispensable to his own team manager, and he also actively responded to the client and other team managers. He stepped in when a couple of other managers were underperforming, not answering their own team members' questions or those of the clients, so he became aware of problems and delays in the user interface team and the front-end team.

Through all these interactions, Steve developed a broad understanding of the project and the status of all the teams. He also earned the client's trust through all his backchannel assistance, and in their private DMs he pitched this change to the client several times. The first few times, the client insisted on proposing the change to the other managers (who declined because they didn't know the framework), but eventually the client lost confidence in the managers who were underperforming or not being responsive, and he trusted Steve's ability to deliver the whole project with the change in framework that Steve favored. The communication network changed even more dramatically following that change—most communication then flowed to and through Steve and Steve's original manager, who supported the change but never developed quite as much power as Steve.

Networks of Managers

This situation illustrates a shift of formal authority, and it turned out to be the basic pattern we observed for how managers develop influence in flash organizations. After we ran three large 30-person flash "organizations" (teams of teams), we visualized the communication network among everyone involved based on their Slack messages. We saw that the most influential people in each of the flash organizations had a similar position in the communication network: they had the most and the strongest network ties *with other managers*. (We defined *most influential* by how many decisions they made that other people enacted, and we defined *strength of ties* based on the number of Slack messages with all network partners.) Across all three flash organizations, there were many effective managers who had strong ties within their teams and even with the client. But the most influential people across each flash organization had strong ties with the other managers, too.

After the study was completed, we analyzed the content of the messages of the managers (with their permission) to see what further insights we could gain. We reviewed their messages with the clients, the managers, and their trusted team members. The content of their private messages (again, shared with us by them for our learnings after the study) revealed how much time the managers spent on both planning and repair. Even when a client gave a high-level idea of what they wanted built, there needed to be many more specific decisions about how different teams would work on building their part of the project, and how they would collaborate with each other as they did so. For example, determining how the software would receive a user's screen interactions, and what kind of data and response it would return, were key decision points. Even knowing in the abstract what needs to happen, the different teams had to decide exactly how those integrations across teams will work. In these larger flash organizations that we studied, the managers would convene backchannel meetings to flesh out all of those decisions. The more backchannel meetings they attended, the better their perspective and overall vantage point for knowing how to communicate with anyone across the organization about what was happening.

We saw that the influential managers had the best understanding of what was happening across the organization. They knew the client's concerns, they knew the true status of other teams based on conversations with the other managers, and they knew what was happening within their own team.

We'll talk much more later in the chapter about all of the repair work the managers were doing. Here, we'll focus on how networks of managers accomplished this adaptive change, and what made them successful in this effort.

Activating the Relevant Network of Managers

A study we conducted in a different setting illustrates the important point that an entire network of managers can help an organization dynamically adapt. We studied the work of two leaders and their teams at a large academic medical center as they tried to drive extensive organization change in the setting of cancer care.

The two leaders—Kate Surman, a consultant, and Sri Seshardri, an executive at the medical center—had a network of leaders whom they trusted. Their strategy for driving change was what they called "connecting the dots"—figuring out who needs to be in the planning discussions and who manages specific changes as the organization adapts together. Here is a small but typical example: Surman and Seshardri encountered unexpected water in the basement of a new building that had recently opened. Water is clearly an urgent situation, because even an isolated crisis is likely to impact numerous groups within the organization. Per their typical pattern, they immediately started to figure out who needed to be notified. The problem involved many managers, from registration and operations to imaging and construction, and those specific managers needed to be on scene playing an active role in planning a collective response.

They needed to "connect the dots," and within a very few minutes they had done so, and the group of the relevant managers was standing in a circle in this basement room, planning what every single group would need to do to deal with the situation.

What is the purpose of "connecting the dots" like this? Or said another way, why will you need to find the relevant network of managers to help drive change?

The reason has to do with how complex organizational change can be. We saw over and over in this cancer center study and in our flash teams studies that a change in one team will have upstream and downstream and adjacent effects on many other teams. A lab sped up their throughput time considerably, but then they overran the clinics who were not ready for the patients to be discharged from the lab so efficiently. Or an IT team improved a feature in the registration team's software but did not anticipate that the code they changed was connected to the code that automatically printed a discharge form for a clinic team.

Across all of these examples, someone had to figure out the full set of managers whose local teams needed to adapt for the overall global change to actually work. Back to the managers standing together in the basement—the operations manager offers one idea on how to deal with the unexpected water, and the registration manager is on hand to know how that idea would impact patient flow. That's the power of connecting the dots.

Renegotiating Managers' Commitments

There's one more step to in this overall process of activating the relevant network of managers for change. Once all of the relevant managers are in the loop (which is hard to do!), you need to then figure out what exactly they and their teams need to do in support of the overall change.

Kate Surman, the consultant in our cancer center study, has a framework of questions to help managers become clear on what they are committing to in a changing situation. She simply, clearly, and directly asks whether the manager can commit to a new obligation. For example: "Can you deliver an extra screen on the mobile app with no extra days on the timeline?" "Can you add a machine learning analysis with no extra team members?" The point is to ask them directly to take on a very specific new goal.[1]

When asked to commit to a specific new goal, the managers really started to think. They started to deeply and specifically envision what it would take to accomplish that goal. "There's no way that I could do an extra screen with no extra days . . . [thinking face] . . . unless. . . ." And then they might have a creative idea or a brainstorm and figure out a new way to do it. These questions invariably prompted generative brainstorms on feasibility as well as critical discussions about likely impacts on other upstream and downstream teams. For example, Surman asked the chemotherapy infusion center whether they could commit to a certain patient throughput time. The manager said they would be happy to work toward that but that they were reliant on the lab and the lab timing. So the lab manager would have to meet some specific requirements in order for the infusion center to commit to a specific throughput time.

We saw versions of that conversation over and over. When you ask a manager to imagine meeting a new goal, they need to consider the inputs they're getting from other team as well as the downstream teams who are dependent on them, and they can start to figure out all the other changes that need to take place on other teams in order for them to meet their own new goal. It's the aspirational goal combined with their deep process expertise that prompts these ideas on how to do it.

It's a simple framework: connect the dots and ask each manager to commit to a specific new goal. Within that framework, the network of managers comes to life to handle the needed and complex changes. They anticipate the complex upstream and downstream effects of their own changes and negotiate a collective plan for change.

We illustrated the framework first based on the cancer center study, but this framework is exactly what we saw happen virtually in the best-performing flash teams. Some new piece of information would come in, and the managers would immediately start messaging each other on Slack to connect the dots and figure out how the plans needed to change.

When Mark's ambulance app prototype, discussed in chapter 1, was first put in the hands of actual EMTs as users, they immediately said that they needed two different workflows: one for acute cases and one for non-acute cases. This feedback makes sense, but had not been part of Mark's initial plans. Quickly, the manager of the Android team who had become the de facto leader of the organization (in fact, she had a linking pin position) messaged each team manager to ask them to propose changes to their team's work to respond to this new feedback. She connected the dots and kept doing so. Together the network of managers anticipated many of the needed changes as they adapted to the client's new requirement, and they discovered and responded to many more needed changes on the fly.

Avoiding the Dark Sides of Hierarchy

We spent a lot of time in these two chapters talking about how hierarchy can facilitate adaptive teams. But we know that the word *hierarchy* is just as likely to make you think of arrogant or disrespectful superiors, or of a structural resistance to change, as it is to make you think of dynamic teams. Let's talk about why that is, and how to get the coordination boost that hierarchy offers while avoiding the stifling, inhibiting, or demoralizing dynamics that can come with hierarchy.

Valentine's office neighbor is Bob Sutton, an organizational psychologist who has made a career of studying hierarchy. Bob is the author of famous books on hierarchy gone very wrong, like *The No Asshole Rule*[2] and *Good Boss, Bad Boss*.[3] Assholes and bad bosses aside, Bob actually considers himself a proponent of organizational hierarchy—something he admits only with considerable caveats. He often introduces his positive views on hierarchy as an accidental discovery when he realized that hierarchy is "essential in organizations" and realized "that less isn't better."[4] He tells the story of being raised to view hierarchy as bad by a father who ranted against the idiocy of bureaucracy and the toxicity of top-down control. Somehow that sentiment seems to permeate Silicon Valley, where we live and work, as well. There is a famous mostly true story of Larry Page, a founder of Google, setting up 100 engineers to report to a single executive (i.e., no middle managers) in an attempt to make Google function like a small company without hierarchy. It didn't work. As Bob explains, "without those middle managers, it was nearly impossible for people to do their work and for executives to grasp and influence what was happening in the company. Page learned the hard way that a hierarchy can be too flat and that middle managers are often a necessary complexity."[5]

We share Bob's conclusion that hierarchy is inevitable and essential and that the work is to create hierarchies that work well. Bob's encouragement to leaders based on thousands of studies of hierarchy is to focus on making hierarchies that work well, instead of eliminating them, which is impossible.

The key seems to be detangling the dysfunctional dynamics that emerge around an organizational hierarchy from the essential functions. We'll mention two big dysfunctions. The first is that structural hierarchy—meaning who reports to whom on the organizational chart—can get tied together with how people are respected and treated. That's unnecessary and demoralizing. The second is that structural hierarchy can be enacted in a way that protects the status quo and makes people's work harder. If there is a chain of command and every link in the chain adds another non-trivial chance for a good idea to get squashed, then yes: the hierarchy will perpetuate a less-than-ideal status quo.

How to disentangle the dysfunction from the essential parts of hierarchy? When it comes to the issues of status and respect, awareness seems a key part. Leaders are the key for modeling cultures of psychological safety and respect.[6] Because it is inevitable and essential, the design challenge is to build a hierarchy that supports coordination and change within complex tasks. That's its only job, coordination and change in service of complex tasks.

10 Practice the Art of Collaborative Repair

"What's happening with the GPS?"

Mark, the doctor from chapter 1 who made the ER/ambulance app, sent this message an uncomfortable number of times before he got something that seemed like an answer.

The app's GPS functionality—by which the screen could visualize the location of an approaching ambulance—was the most challenging feature to bring online. It required novel cross-team cooperation, and for about a week, Mark kept getting "I don't know, ask so-and-so" from various team managers who otherwise seemed very on top of things.

After sending a series of DMs, he figured out that a hardworking but quiet engineer from the front-end team had taken this task on and was working closely with a back-end engineer to figure it out. Mark started messaging actively with this mini-cross-functional team and they figured it out. Soon, the remote engineer in Portugal could see the blue dot on his mobile phone tracking Mark driving up to the emergency room at a hospital in Utah.

In our postmortem reviews of this flash team's Slack DMs, it was almost comical (and humbling as the flash team's sponsors) how many times he had to ask the same question. However, instead of becoming coercive, demanding, or rude, Mark focused on understanding why there was a problem, asking questions focused on understanding, rather than blame. Through this wave of constructive questioning, Mark found the team member who had the expertise and position to fix the novel GPS feature. The team cheered the day the GPS feature started working, and Mark helped the team figure out how to solve his most pressing problem.

When you're working in the world of flash teams, you should expect that things will regularly go wrong. Programs will have bugs, people will have personal emergencies, the internet will go out, and you will certainly have to say "You're muted" in 95 percent of your Zoom meetings. We found that every project we worked on or studied involved at least one major problem and many, many smaller ones. So, to equip you for the future of flash teams, we need to discuss the very human art of learning to repair when you realize that something has gone wrong. Given the importance of expecting and fixing problems, the next two studies we present are about how flash teams managers repaired the problems they encountered.

Collaborative Repair

What you're about to read in this section might be boiled down to the simple observation "don't be a jerk." You might wonder what it's doing in a book about flash teams. Unfortunately, a long line of research has repeatedly demonstrated that we often come across as a jerk when we communicate online, regardless of whether we intend to.[1] We are just not good at estimating how our words come across when stripped of the vocal inflections and other in-person signals that we give off. So we need to address how to handle effective communication effectively with flash teams.

This next lesson comes from a study in which we discovered how differently a range of client managers handled problems they encountered on Upwork. We started out our research with an open question of what made a difference in successful versus failed project engagements. In collaboration with then-PhD student Hatim Rahman, we worked to figure out what made the difference between successful and failed projects on Upwork.[2]

The difference between successful and failed projects was actually not in perfect plans and execution, but in how the client manager responded to inevitable problems. Some of the client managers would ascribe negative intentionality or characteristics to the freelancers when they encountered problems in the projects, and reacted punitively. In contrast, the client managers of the successfully completed projects took a collaborative approach to repair the breaches. They assumed situational causes—"it's the project's fault, not your fault"—and accordingly asked questions to diagnose the cause of the problem and plan a solution in collaboration with the team.

In some ways this sounds obvious, but the application of it seems to go against our nature. Research shows that people tend to interpret disrupting events as "willful and meaningful," which justifies their feeling disturbed, upset, indignant, afraid, or surprised when they encounter a problem.[3] When you're managing a flash team, an orientation towards collaborative repair will be key to ensuring the likelihood of your project success. These kinds of approaches are most effectively modeled by leaders from day one.

The social lesson learned is that when you encounter a problem at work, you're more likely to achieve a successful outcome if you get curious about the situational causes and say, "Let's figure out together what's going on here," rather than assuming that problems are born of someone else's personal failings and saying, "I haven't heard from you, you must be missing a basic moral compass." We wish we were joking here, but honestly some of the direct messages (DMs) we analyzed for this study were pretty intense.

Interestingly, even though this seems like a very socially focused insight, software plays a central role because the managers often carried out their threats and punitive strategies using platform levers. In flash teams, after all, all communication and social interactions are mediated by software and platform features. The clients who took a constructive approach were likely to use the platform's software features to help create understanding and to offer rewards and bonuses to the freelancers. The clients who ascribed problems to personal lapses on the part of a freelancer were likely to instead use the platform's software features to quickly threaten the freelancer with bad ratings and reviews or filing disputes with the platform. The features are there to protect the transaction—people need recourse if work isn't getting done—but our analysis showed that these managers weren't facing any more serious problems or any more problematic freelancers than any other manager. Had they engaged in collaborative repair rather than platform threats, they were likely to have gotten to a successful outcome. It reminds us a bit of car horns. They are actually designed to serve as a safety feature to protect drivers but are often instead used for petty punishments.

The Tactics of Coercive Control

Here are the most distinctive tactics we saw by managers who were coercive or threatening in their approach towards misunderstandings, rather than oriented toward mutual respect and collective good. To repeat ourselves, these are *not* good management. Don't do these.

Threatening payment. Even after making a payment, client managers can request refunds if the work does not meet their expectations. For instance, a client manager hired a contractor to develop a mobile app. After identifying a bug, the manager demanded a $1,500 refund, claiming the contractor introduced the issue. Despite attempts to fix it, the contractor faced continued dissatisfaction and eventually abandoned the project.

This scenario illustrates the coercive control that client managers can exert. Such actions create a hostile work environment, eroding trust and cooperation. The contractor defended their work and attempted to fix the issue, but the client manager remained unsatisfied, leading to the contractor giving up on the project altogether.

Threatening formal disputes. When contractors refused refund requests, some client managers escalated matters by threatening formal disputes with Upwork. These disputes could result in the suspension of the contractor's account, effectively ending the project and straining the manager-contractor relationship. In one case, a client manager hired a contractor to fix app bugs. When the client found the fixes inadequate, they threatened to dispute the $511 payment unless the contractor reworked the bugs without additional compensation. The contractor's attempt to explain the progress was met with a dispute filing, resulting in project termination.

Such a coercive tactic can backfire, as it did in this case. The contractor, feeling unfairly treated, stopped responding, leading to project failure. The threat of disputes creates an environment of fear and resentment, undermining the collaborative spirit necessary for project success.

Threatening ratings. Client managers also used the platform's rating and hiring system coercively. For example, one manager warned a contractor to send updates or face a negative rating and replacement. This approach often led to frustration and project failure, as contractors struggled to meet demands under unjust pressure.

In another instance, a client manager hired a contractor for a software engineering project. After not receiving updates as expected, the client manager threatened to hire someone else, leveraging the potential impact on the contractor's future work. Such threats undermine the contractor's motivation and can lead to disengagement and project failure.

The Tactics of Collaborative Repair

In contrast to these coercive tactics, some client managers adopted a collaborative repair approach. By focusing on task-specific feedback, combining criticism with praise, and sharing responsibility for issues, they pursued mutual and shared understanding and responsibility.

Offering task-focused feedback. Providing specific, non-coercive feedback encouraged contractors to take ownership of errors and remain engaged. For instance, a manager discovered a major bug in a contractor's software submission, but simply highlighted the issue without attributing blame. The contractor quickly fixed the problem and continued working, ensuring project progress and completion.

In another example, a client manager hired a contractor to develop a software program. After the contractor submitted a portion of the project, the client manager reviewed their work and said, "I try not to bother my programmer unnecessarily. But there is a major bug: The user data can never be updated. No matter how many times I run, the .xml file remains the same. And there is just one single record in History."[4] The contractor took responsibility for the "hitch" in the submitted work, was willing to fix the problem, and remained engaged. Upon receiving the next update from the contractor, the client manager commented, "Thanks for the new version. My impression is that it implements all that I wanted. And the program is now working."[5] This approach gave the contractor a chance to fix the work without the threat of losing the project or receiving a negative rating, ultimately contributing to continued compliance and project completion.

Coupling criticism with praise. Combining criticism with praise softened the impact of negative feedback and maintained contractor morale. In one case, a client manager thanked a contractor for their hard work on a mobile app before mentioning issues with the app not displaying correctly when the phone was turned sideways into landscape mode. The contractor explained the complexity and offered solutions, resulting in continued collaboration and successful project delivery.

For instance, a client manager encountered major issues with a mobile application and responded, "Thank you so much for your hard work on this :) ... But I noticed some issues with landscape mode. Like if I turn the phone to landscape mode, the views are all jumbled. Do you know what is causing that issue? Also, I'm really having trouble understanding the code unfortunately. Where do I replace the URL of the web service if I want a different web server? Can you be very specific on what file I have to change? Also, where are the incoming received messages being parsed? What file should I look for?"[6]

The contractor responded by detailing why the client manager encountered issues with the program in landscape mode and offered a way to address additional problems. The contractor also committed to providing more clearly documented code. The client manager appreciated the response, replying, "AWESOME! Thank you :) Please take the time that you need. Thank you so much for your hard work!!"[7]

With new, shared expectations of how to work together, the contractor continued to work on the project, and the manager was ultimately pleased with the final submitted work.

Shared responsibility. Taking shared responsibility for problems fosters mutual respect and collaboration. One client manager hired a contractor to develop a computational text-analysis program that automatically read and processed certain texts. After reviewing the contractor's progress, the client manager not only asked about and suggested "alternative methods" to address the problem, but also took the blame for "missing something obvious" in the submitted work.[8] The contractor provided a detailed explanation related to the client manager's questions. Additionally, the contractor asked specifically about near-term changes the client manager wanted.

The client manager and contractor continued to engage in collaborative discussions and align their expectations of how to work together. This client manager even paid the contractor a bonus upon project completion. In general, we observed that some client managers engaged in the project's nitty-gritty, subtly encouraging contractors to immerse themselves more fully in the project as well. Seeing managers willing to engage with them without the threat of using Upwork's tools coercively, contractors voluntarily engaged in joint problem solving and brainstorming.

Notably, these collaborative repair tactics led to more successful projects, and also often led to continued interactions beyond the project's end. In fact, this result reminded us of a comment from Taurean Dyer, the engineer from Accenture who ran a successful flash team. Dyer said he was surprised by how passionate and driven the contractors who he worked with were. He told us, "You can really get so much out of your workers if you give them what they actually want to do and give them the work and freedom that gives them a chance to shine." He recalled with a laugh the energizing long hours and sprints that he would do with his flash team, where he's thinking to himself, "I want you to go to sleep, because I want to go to sleep. But I also think it is amazing that you're willing to do this work with me."

We saw this over and over in the study. Managers who offered upfront payments or extended contracts signaled trust and appreciation, resulting in ongoing cooperation and enjoyment of each other. For instance, after resolving initial misunderstandings, a manager offered upfront payment, leading to significant progress and project completion. Another manager left a perfect rating and opened a new contract for the contractor, reinforcing a positive working relationship. We saw another example where the client manager and contractor worked through a misunderstanding and continued on the project. The client manager reached out to the contractor, "Let me know ANYTIME if you want any amount of upfront payment, and I will send it to you immediately."[9]

Backstage Repair: Fixing Problems Behind the Scenes

The examples above came from direct interactions between clients and contractors. When it comes to change and repair, you should also expect that there will be private conversations behind the scenes in your flash organization. It is very human and very healthy to take some space to privately solve problems, in what's called the *backstage*. We were able to get permission from the managers of several of our flash teams to analyze their private direct messages to each other, well after the study was over and well after they had all been paid. With this additional insight into the functioning of these flash teams, we saw a new and important pattern: whenever a problem arose, the managers retreated to their DMs (on private Slack channels) with trusted collaborators to solve them.

It might be tempting to think that, if all your flash team managers are coordinating behind the scenes with each other, there might be a communication problem with your flash team. But the examples we'll share demonstrate that private, candid interactions in backstage repairs lead to managers having a more realistic understanding of progress and problems. They also created solidarity and trust among those who made it into the backstage repair conversations. This study of these interactions shows how much power and authority can grow outside formal settings, often as a side effect of this kind of backstage repair work. We saw that the managers who engaged in more backstage repairs developed and maintained more authority in their flash organizations.

Here are some examples from flash teams we've worked with. In one case, despite their strong ethic of respecting artists and artistic creativity, a flash team's leaders found themselves unhappy with the content they received from the artists on their team. In a private discussion with one of the writers, the clients expressed their dilemma of not wanting to overtly manage the artistic process. The writer quietly began to adapt the other artists' work to be usable in the project, allowing her to assign work to herself and a select few writers whose styles aligned with the clients' vision. This repair to the process happened entirely without public discussion or conflict, ensuring the group's sense of a smooth operation. As another example, a team member once accidentally shared incorrect information in the public channel. A manager moved the conversation to a private channel, advising the team member to delete the message. This swift backstage repair maintained professionalism and prevented the client from seeing the error.

These backstage interactions not only ensured smooth operations but also built a strong relationship between managers and team members. We saw in our analysis that backstage repairs fostered solidarity—those who engaged in backstage repairs helped each other avoid slips and failures and public critiques. The backstage interactions also involved more joking and humor. These kinds of informal interactions might be especially important for developing cohesion and solidarity in these on-demand teams.

How to Be a Bad Flash Team Manager

We developed the idea of collaborative repair to explain how good managers respond to unexpected situations and surprises. All the other business books tell you how to be a good boss. We get the vision, but we also see some wisdom as we experiment with flash teams—with their quick hiring, remote work, and AI management tools—to review in the short term how you avoid being a bad boss. Here we'll cover some common pitfalls.

The most common mistake is to view the worker as a distant service. In fact, the most negative feedback we've ever gotten from someone running a flash team was that it felt empty, essentially "set it and forget it." This leader did not communicate with the workers and was not involved in the team. This is wrong, and it's a recipe for both bad results and demoralized workers. Don't do this.

It makes sense why this might be tempting with flash teams: the workers are not in the same building as you, they don't walk by your water cooler, and they may not know anyone else on your team. They may not even be working at the same time you are, if they're located overseas. Pamela Hinds of Stanford University has documented thoroughly how remote workers can be out of sync with the rest of their teams. As she demonstrates, this can even lead to increased conflict with other team members.[10]

Instead, good flash team managers make sure to check in with their workers regularly. This isn't rocket science, and it would be viewed as table stakes in a traditional organization—do it with flash teams too. If you want to catch problems before they escalate, you need to build up communication lines and trust with the workers. If you want to make sure you don't wind up with a car sales voiceover pitch for your research paper, like the one we described in chapter 1, you need to check in early to make sure that expectations are aligned.

The second common mistake is to underpay. On some platforms, the problem is prevalent enough that it constitutes wage theft. It's best to start from a point of view that workers are making an honest effort to do what you asked. If a worker is underperforming, consider this perspective. We recommend refusing to make payment only if you have evidence that the worker is actively scamming you. If the worker is putting in an effort, they deserve to be paid fairly.

One of the reasons why payment is such a touchy subject is that there aren't widely shared norms for payment of flash team workers. There are some workers on these platforms who work for extremely low wages. The minimum wage supported on Upwork is a measly three dollars an hour. Should you pay these low wages, even if the cost of living for that worker is low? Should you instead pay minimum wage in your home jurisdiction? Somewhere in between? M. Six Silberman and collaborators have spent years navigating these thorny issues, as both local and federal governments around the world begin to regulate them.[11] We'll discuss more on this in chapter 18.

The third common mistake is to not communicate. Workers themselves in these spaces often want to communicate in detail and carefully—to *over-communicate*—in order to make sure that they do exactly what they want. They are managing up because they want you to be happy with the result. (Keep in mind that their reputation on the platform is dependent on your five-star rating, so they want to please you.) In fact, Brian McInnis and colleagues at Cornell University studied an online worker forum, finding that workers veered away from any task that felt like it might risk a bad rating or an unpaid rejection of their work.[12]

Think of it this way: imagine that you were a chef, and you just got an order for a hamburger. But you don't know anything more than that. Maybe the hamburger is supposed to be gourmet, or maybe it's for a five-year-old who will scream bloody murder if there's anything besides bun and meat on the plate. Or maybe it's supposed to be a vegetarian burger. Do they want it well done or medium rare? As a gourmet chef, you know that there are many options available. The customer who ordered the hamburger didn't think to specify those options, and they may not even have been aware that they exist. But you know that if you give the customer something other than what they want, the hamburger's getting sent back and you're not getting paid.

So what are you, the chef, to do? If you get an order that doesn't have all the details, you need to go back and ask the customer. This is what online workers will often do. They know all of the decision points, since they are experts, and you probably do not. So, they are faced with the question of making a decision without your input and hoping that it's the right one, or communicating with you to get clarification. Our observation is that online workers will often err toward communication, which is a gift to the project outcomes.

11 Navigating Worker Voice and Client Voice

Adam Marcus felt the weight of his message for the experts at the company's internal town hall meeting. These virtual meetings offer a space for copywriters, designers, and other professionals to connect with staff and hear about the latest updates, tools, and project highlights. Today, though, his company B12 was rolling out machine-drafted blog posts in the websites that they designed for customers, which meant that the copywriters in their expert network were becoming copy editors, and the amount of time they would spend on any one project would be going down.

Marcus is B12's founder and CTO. B12 coordinates experts' on-demand contributions to build websites for their customers. They assembled teams from among a large network of freelance experts and managed their contributions using a lot of automation on a smart platform system they developed called Orchestra.

Marcus was proud of their town halls and the positive relationship B12 maintained with their network of experts. They encouraged two-way communication with the freelance experts and used the town halls to highlight successful projects and answer questions about how things were going.

They knew there would be concerns and questions about the machine-drafted blog posts. They worked to distill the change into one slide that was both empathetic and factual to what they expected to happen. Marcus and his team wanted to avoid euphemisms, knowing people see through those. They also didn't want to assume what was good or bad. Some might prefer being copy editors over copywriters.

What they could offer, thanks to a lot of testing, was a clear answer on how much more efficient the process would be, and how much less time they'd need for each project. They had already prototyped the new workflow, so they could confidently outline the two major changes that the expert freelancers would experience. Marcus later reflected, "If you're going to introduce this technology, you have to help people understand it and digest it. Interpreting and communicating the impact of the technology is one of the more challenging aspects of fairly deploying this work."

Flash teams are an opportunity to think creatively and deliberately about relationships between people. Some of the focus will be on the dynamic project-based teams. But some of the focus can be on the network of experts who might come together for any of those projects. How healthy and connected is that community? You might be a leader, participant, or client of such communities, but in all cases, you'll be invested in whether that community is thriving.

We've encountered many different networks or communities over the years of doing this work. They differ in size, age, areas of expertise, and location. Some of these networks of contributors are volunteer initiatives, such as Wikipedia, which organizes a huge international community of editors, contributors, and yes, bots. Some of these networks are paid marketplaces, such as Upwork, which has a large headquarters in California that creates and oversees an international market of diverse experts. We have found it notable and important that across many, many examples, these large groups coalesce into a coherent social community of sorts, with notable group dynamics.

We'll tell you about a few of those examples, focusing on a topic of much interest to contractors today—algorithmic ratings, which are systems defined and managed by the owners of the platforms that are curating the network.

Caring for the Communities That Enable Flash Teams

In our work, we get to meet the leaders of many of these communities, and it was interesting to us that some of their proudest moments came through interactions with the larger community. Adam Marcus, for example, in the story above, highlighted the importance of two-way communication through their expert town halls.

The town halls provided more than just information dissemination. Marcus notes that they add a layer of humanity to what could otherwise feel like a piecework operation. Each meeting showcases recent work completed by experts, recognizing their contributions and providing an opportunity for back-and-forth discussions about what's working and what could be improved. This approach helps build a strong sense of inclusion and recognition among the experts, making them feel more connected to the company and their role in its success.

Pat Petitti, cofounder of the consulting network Catalant, also brought up the idea of community support when reflecting on the contribution Catalant had made. Catalant had made a deliberate shift towards supporting smaller communities within the large network of business consultants they curated. He and cofounder Rob Biederman were energized by their engagements with the community. They also held town halls, offering consultants a transparent view into Catalant's strategy, the projects they're tackling, and the company's future direction. They use the town halls to foster a sense of community and partnership, ensuring that its consultants feel valued and included, even as they maintain the independence that drew them to the platform in the first place.

Both B12 and Catalant recognize the power of direct communication and feedback. Marcus shared how B12's introduction of automated project staffing emerged from conversations in these town halls. Freelancers voiced concerns about balancing autonomy in project selection with the efficiency of automation. Some wanted more control over their project choices, while others valued the predictability and ease of automatic assignments. Through this process, B12 was able to address concerns transparently, ensuring that all parties understood how the system worked and could make informed decisions about participation.

These examples illustrate the alchemy of community and flexibility that emerge in these contractor networks. By prioritizing regular communication and fostering a strong sense of connection, companies like B12, Catalant, Flash Hub, and Gigster enable their networks of experts to thrive. Such dynamics are also available and important in large firms that might be attempting more flash-like models within their own workforces. When the community is thriving, the members of a flash team can come together and focus on their collaborative projects in deeply engaged and empowered ways.

Algorithmic Ratings in Online Networks and Labor Markets

We'll now dive deeper into the functionality of a common tool that companies use to manage these large communities of contractors—algorithmic ratings. These rating systems can have massive impacts on how your community feels about their work environment.

Algorithmic ratings are a central data-driven tool for managing work, especially in gig work and online labor markets. If you have used Lyft or Uber for rides or DoorDash for food delivery, their systems have probably asked you to rate the workers. Similarly, online expert labor markets such as Upwork will collect client ratings and other data to calculate and display algorithmic ratings on the profiles of their contractors. The impact of these ratings largely depends on how platforms, managers, and companies enact them.

The general idea is that in online labor markets, or other kinds of gig work, you rely on algorithmic ratings because you are not personally familiar with the contractor, and you don't know their reputation among your network of collaborators. The ratings themselves, in turn, rely heavily on feedback from previous clients who have hired the worker, or other performance data. Platform companies vary in how much detail they provide on the data that are used or the calculations that go into the ratings.

Consider, for your own work, how comfortable you would feel having an AI-driven rating system determine the income or work you will be getting in the future. As you can imagine, the more automated approaches evoke a fraught debate for many workers, because it directly and materially affects their livelihood. Jobs are won and lost based on it. Min Kyung Lee and others at Carnegie Mellon University interviewed a number of drivers for ridesharing platforms about their experiences with algorithms and AIs determining their reputation on the platforms.[1] They reported how the algorithm doesn't know or care why things go wrong: if a driver declines to take a customer, even if for safety reasons, it counts against their rating. Sometimes, riders would give them low ratings for reasons entirely out of their control, like traffic jams, surge pricing leading to an unexpectedly costly ride, or GPS errors. Many others have likewise detailed how reputation systems can dramatically shape the anxieties and behaviors of workers on these platforms.[2]

Let's now look at three studies that explored how algorithmic ratings play out in different labor markets and client communities.

Dealing with Rating Inflation

The average ratings on most platforms are quite high. Why is that? If it's true that, as Upwork advertises on its homepage, the average client rating is 4.9 out of 5, is there really any meaningful signal if everyone gives 4.9 or 5.0 out of 5?

John Horton at MIT termed this phenomenon *reputation inflation*. He studied a dataset from a large online marketplace over a ten-year period and found that the proportion of ratings between 1 and 4.99 remained constant or fell in that time, while the proportion of 5-star reviews increased from roughly 33 percent of ratings at the beginning of the decade to nearly 90 percent of ratings at the end of the decade.[3] To repeat: *ninety percent of ratings are five star!* Horton also looked at other metrics that were not visible to users of the platform to see if the quality of work had correspondingly improved in that time, but alas, it was not the case: the ratings were improving, but the work wasn't. Instead, platform users were responding to social pressure, for example to just be a nice person and help out the worker, especially since there was no cost to the platform users themselves for giving a higher rating.

This probably happens to you all the time: when you use Instacart, Doordash, or other delivery platforms, the software probably constantly pesters you for ratings. "Why shouldn't I give this worker a top rating?" you think to yourself. "They brought the food to me fine, and I don't even think I could define what makes a four-star delivery vs. a five-star delivery. I don't want to hurt their career. Here you go, five stars." And if there does happen to be a small issue, you are more likely not to leave a rating at all rather than harm the worker by tattling on them to the platform.

This is the entirely reasonable process that leads to everyone getting five-star ratings. The problem is that this prosocial tendency to be a good person and leave top ratings will then make the ratings themselves less useful for future clients. These platforms become a real-life Lake Wobegon, where "all the children are above average." We all know the statistical impossibility of everyone being above average, yet when 90 percent of ratings are the top possible score, there's not much we can do about it. Researchers have spent years trying to improve these reputation systems for these platforms. One solution developed by a global collaboration of scholars involves a boomerang effect of sorts, so that if you give someone a good rating, they get earlier access to your next job.[4] Imagine how it might change your behavior if the next time you give an Uber driver five stars, they become more likely to show up at your doorstep the next time you need a ride—you'd be much more inclined to be honest about the quality of their work.

Depending on the platform, though, you may not have to worry too much about this. For one, in many contexts, the difference between someone who rates a 4.6 and someone who rates a 4.7 may not matter to you—for example, as long as your groceries get to you on time, it's fine. Second, platforms often find ways to compensate for rating inflation. This is why, for example, platforms such as Upwork will identify "expert-vetted" workers (their top 1 percent, manually screened) or "top talent" to further differentiate the crème de la crème from others who have good ratings. Some platforms will also smooth over ratings: if someone only has one rating and it's one star, it probably doesn't make sense for the platform to directly show that one rating—a more likely situation is that the worker may be slightly below average, but definitely not as bad as someone else who repeatedly only gets one-star ratings.[5]

So, the most important thing to pay attention to is whether the platform you're using has enacted any of these processes. If not, buyer beware: someone's rating may be driven by a very small number of very happy (or very unhappy) previous engagements.

What does this have to do with worker voice and wellbeing? Well, it turns out that client and platform responses to this rating problem can create serious consequences for workers. Read on.

The Negative Consequences of Opaque or Unpredictable Algorithmic Ratings

Hatim Rahman of Northwestern University studied an online labor market that initially used a simple and public-facing rating system, where clients rated projects on a scale of 1 to 5 on dimensions such as skills, communication, and quality. The platform aggregated clients' scores on each dimension to provide an overall evaluation score for each project and then aggregate project scores to create the overall rating for each contractor.[6] Rahman's study took a pivotal turn when the platform shifted to a largely opaque algorithm to create the rating instead, in an effort to combat the rampant rating inflation on the platform. Unlike traditional work evaluations, where criteria are clear and feedback is accessible, the workers pointed out that the opaque ratings obscured the criteria for success. The opacity prevented workers from understanding how to improve their ratings, leading to frustration and even paranoia among some. Workers couldn't determine which of their actions influenced their scores and lived in a perpetual state of uncertainty.

There were several aspects of the algorithmic rating system that contributed to the unpredictability experienced by the workers. First, although the evaluation criteria were opaque, it was also evident to workers that the evaluation criteria were constantly shifting, leaving them unsure about what specific actions would impact their ratings. For example, a worker might complete multiple projects successfully but see their rating fluctuate without understanding why. Second, the platform did not make clear the intervals at which new evaluations and rating calculations would occur; they did not know when their actions would be reviewed or when changes in their scores might be evident. One freelancer described completing several tasks in the hope of boosting his rating but found that the algorithm updated sporadically, sometimes weeks or months later.

The magnitude of changes also remained unclear to workers. For instance, minor mistakes might lead to disproportionately large drops in ratings, while significant successes might not result in expected improvements. It was also unclear to workers how the feedback from various parties was weighted. For example, a worker might receive positive feedback from a client but see no improvement in their rating, suggesting that the platform's internal metrics play a more significant role than they realize.

Workers on the platform adopted strategies to cope with the opacity of the ratings. High performers who were highly dependent on the platform for their income and who experienced setbacks in their ratings often increased their activity on the platform, trying different approaches to boost their visibility and ratings.[7] For example, some might take on a wider variety of projects or change their work habits in hopes of discovering what actions would lead to higher scores. Conversely, high performers who did not experience setbacks, or those less dependent on the platform, tended to limit their platform engagement, avoiding actions that could potentially lower their ratings.[8] They often played it safe, taking on fewer projects and sticking to well-established methods they believed were less likely to negatively affect their scores. This cautious approach was seen as a way to minimize risk in an unpredictable system.

Low performers, on the other hand, often displayed a more diverse set of reactive behaviors. With less to lose and a greater need to improve their standing, they were more likely to experiment with a broader range of tactics. This could include accepting projects outside their usual categories or trying different ways to complete tasks, all in an effort to discover any possible means of improving their ratings. If the system seems random and stochastic, then being random and stochastic yourself is a reasonable response!

If you are hiring and managing flash teams, then the lesson is clear: set clear and transparent evaluation criteria, and stick to them. Failing to do so will lead your workers to react in unpredictable ways as they try to shore up their uncertainty and divine how the evaluations actually work. This is true both of the platform you use to hire, and of how you yourself give ratings. Be up front with the workers: what matters to you, and what doesn't? Maybe you don't care about them being present at meetings as long as they get their work done, or maybe you really need to get regular virtual face time with them. Set the rules of the game and make them clear!

Doing It Better: The Case of Karma

The previous section looked at the downside of algorithmically driven rating systems. However, there are also other communities where AI-based performance approaches worked far better than expected. Valentine collaborated with then-Stanford PhD student Katharina Lix to study Gigster's AI-based evaluation system. Gigster built flash teams of software engineers out of a network of over 800 freelancers in order to create software solutions for clients.[9] Every new project spun up a flash team. We studied this company for over 18 months.

At Gigster, every worker was assigned a rating score called "karma." In order to get hired for development jobs, you needed to raise your karma score. Perhaps learning the lesson from the opaque rating system that we described in the last section, Gigster had an internal company wiki that made it extremely clear what earned or docked karma: delivering a software milestone on time or earning high customer satisfaction ratings increased karma, and failing either of those criteria reduced karma. Workers could also award karma to their coworkers as a token of appreciation for chores like filling in documentation or implementing a boring part of the software. The code for calculating karma was open source, and every worker at the company could see it. The policies were also publicly documented. There was a public karma leaderboard at the company that everyone working there could see.

For these new workers, karma served as their Rosetta Stone, enabling them to make sense of what was happening at the company and who to trust. They learned that the staffers deciding who to hire for each position paid attention to karma, publishing minimum karma requirements for each job and hiring based on karma. As one told us, "It was very clear [how to get good work]: you get karma, you get gigs. [. . .] there was a clear path forward for you. [. . .] Now [working full-time at a technology company], I don't have that. I don't really know how management decides who gets to work on what."[10] The peer karma awards helped team members reward each other or occasionally regulate each other's behavior. The workers felt that this was a productive dynamic: "The result was good. People across the whole network were just working more as a team."[11] Karma also served as a status symbol within Gigster. As one worker described it: "People respected you if you had a high karma score, even if they didn't know anything else about you [. . .] People were really proud of that because [a high karma score meant] you've been around for a while. [If you had a high karma score,] what you said on Slack mattered, people listened to you."[12]

Despite this success, Gigster decided to get rid of karma. It caused a lot of trouble for the company. To understand why, we have to start by recognizing that workers at Gigster operate in a world of far more uncertainty than a traditional job. Workers told us that they were "on their own" and in the "wild west" when they first joined Gigster: they had no clue how to be competitive for new positions.[13] The workers also faced considerable uncertainty about which kinds of jobs they could realistically be competitive for, and whom to trust when they saw messages with advice on how to navigate the system posted in workers' Slack channels.

Ultimately, karma worked because people felt like it reduced uncertainties in a way that they could understand. Even if it had undesirable behaviors, like occasionally debiting karma from workers because the client forgot to mark a deliverable as submitted, overall they felt like it operated by clear rules and treated all freelancers equally. Minimum karma requirements for jobs were clearly visible: there were no hidden criteria for hiring.

The karma system provides evidence that algorithmic management, despite all its flaws, can be attractive when it feels clearer and fairer than other ways of rating workers. As one worker put it, human managers "can't be trusted because they're biased, they have favorites. They change how they make decisions without telling you why, and they don't treat everyone the same."[14] Likewise, Bernstein, a team of Stanford students, and Amy X. Zhang at the University of Washington found that AI judgments are viewed most positively for deciding based on logic and data, whereas people hold suspicions that even experts apply their own beliefs and agenda.[15]

Here's the takeaway: clear, simple algorithms are your best strategy. Clarity makes workers aware of exactly what they need to do to get reviewed well. It also lends legitimacy to an evaluation system. Finally, it can boost motivation by reducing uncertainty and giving them a sense of control over their outcomes. It's when the algorithm is hidden, difficult to discern, or inconsistent that problems arise. Of course, you may need special cases to handle unusual situations, but all else equal, opt for simple and clear algorithms.

And then, zooming back out, algorithmic ratings are a tool that companies use to manage a large network of contractors. This means that they are tools for managing work *relationships* where all parties have a stake in how they are used. Algorithmic technologies can support coordination at scale and can enable a flexible workforce. The experience and outcomes depend on how they are framed, designed, and used. Remember that all of these tools are part of mutual reciprocal relationships; they're best when everyone feels respected and seen and helped in the context of these communities and in the use of these tools.

11 The Future of Flash Teams: Supercharging Your Teams with AI

12 Getting the Right Team in a Flash with AI Hiring

Sal needed a team built around her superstar marketing lead. He's great, Sal thought, but he can't pull off the whole project by himself. Due to a critical client need, Sal had to find a way to get the project done at high quality, and soon.

Sal opened Foundry and started a new flash team. She added her marketing lead to the team, and then listed an overall budget and deadline. Foundry flared to life with suggestions. The suggestions included people who had worked well with the marketing lead on past projects, had complementary expertise of each other, and were collectively within budget. Foundry labeled each person with a percentage indicating how likely it thought the person would be available if asked.

Sal clicked around to explore the recommended teams, then quickly asked her marketing lead for any feedback. Based on his feedback, Sal selected one of the options and, holding her breath, clicked "Recruit." Soon, the faces of the suggested team members started filling in with confirmed workers. As she did, the remaining spaces in the team shifted to new people who were especially likely to collaborate well with those who had already been confirmed. In a few hours, the team was ready to begin.

So far in this book, we have argued that being able to hire experts in minutes is game changing for teams. But we've still been talking about hiring experts one at a time. What if your flash team platform could intelligently hire entire teams at once, using a team hiring algorithm that was informed by your priorities around members' prior experience together, availability before the deadline, expertise, and working styles? A hiring process that is team-optimized and team-aware is an even more powerful lens on convening flash teams, and it becomes possible with the right data and AI tools.

That is the kind of forward thinking and AI focus that we turn to in part II of the book. Flash teams run on software, which means each flash team produces extremely valuable data on their work together—who was hired, what the starting structure was, how that structure evolved over time, and how the group ultimately performed. This data can be fine-grained, learning from subtle signals like single lines of chat, all the way out to more project-level variables like overall role structure and team performance. The point is this: your data set becomes a treasure trove of insights that, coupled with AI, can give your future teams superpowers.

This second part of the book paints the picture of what is likely to come down the pike with flash teams, and the teaming and management superpowers that they may offer. The opportunities in this part of the book will rely on software that isn't widely available yet; we've developed and tested this software in our labs at Stanford or met companies that are developing and innovating it as we write. Yet, even as some of these data-driven and algorithmic approaches are developing, our core argument in part II of the book is this: if you build your organization around flash team capabilities today, you will be positioned better than anyone else in the world to capitalize on these opportunities as they take shape in the next few years.

Artificial Intelligence and the Future of Management

Management, including hiring decisions and team design decisions, can be thought of as an art or a craft—meaning managers make most of their managerial decisions and interventions based on their intuition.[1] Simply because of the state of the management "science," managers lack strong evidence about the likely impact of their decisions, and also currently lack the ability to robustly assess the impact of their decisions through closed feedback loops. Because flash teams automatically generate data on their work processes and related outcomes, they can enable leaders to make more rigorous decisions about hiring and team design and then dynamically learn over time. Leaders equipped with this kind of data-driven reflection have the feedback loops that empower their future flash teams to automatically leverage the learnings from the flash teams of today.

One of the major revolutions of the last decade has been the integration of data science and AI into nearly every industry and aspect of life. The combination of data and AI offer what we think are some compelling and almost unfair advantages to flash teams over those of traditional teams. Consider:

- What if your team could evolve dynamically, with AI guiding you to add fresh perspectives or adjust strategies in real-time—how might that transform the way you work together?
- If you could see exactly what made a project successful—the key roles, workflows, and collaboration styles—how would you use that knowledge to build an even better team?
- If you could pinpoint the tasks that caused delays or needed extra collaboration in a struggling project, how would you redesign your team or process to avoid those issues next time?
- If you could test-drive different team structures—adjusting roles, workflows, and even personalities—before launching your team, how much more confident would you feel about its success?

It's time to take a close look at the emerging AI tools that can help leaders with these kinds of AI-augmented hiring and design decisions that produce superpowered flash teams. We'll start with the story from the start of the chapter—how can AI help you with team-optimized hiring?

When AI Can Help You Hire Entire Teams

You can think of flash teams assembly software as you would a search engine. We want to automatically recruit experts who fill our needed roles, but we also want to have an eye on availability, how much we've worked together, time zone overlap, diversity, and any other recruiting goals we care to set. Let's call each of these goals an *objective* for the flash teams assembly software. With flash teams, there's typically not just one objective that you want. Instead, you probably need the flash teams assembly software to balance many objectives simultaneously. Luckily, AI excels at combining multiple objectives under uncertainty like this.

There are two categories of objectives in recruiting a flash team: objectives around individual workers, and objectives around the collective team. *Individual objectives* are search criteria that you care about when picking each team member: objectives that only care about that worker, not who else is on the team. *Team objectives* are search criteria that you care about when deciding which individuals ought to work together.

Because all of these objectives and scores can be sourced automatically, an algorithm can put them all together to find the team that you're looking for. You hand off your objectives to the AI, and the AI takes it from there. It may not look like the generative AI that you've seen in the news, but searching through huge decision spaces to find the best solution efficiently is exactly the kind of thing that AI techniques have been developed to do well. You might remember the headlines when AI started beating grandmasters at the games of chess and Go—these AIs basically execute huge searches over sets of possible moves.

Individual Objectives

As noted above, individual objectives are the qualities you look for when recruiting single members. The three most important to recruiters are typically skill, cost, and availability. How good is this worker at the skill I need them for? How much do they cost? Are they available when I need them?

An employee's skill level is usually indicated by their reputation rating. The platforms recognize this and typically integrate some sort of reputation system similar to the star ratings you'd see on platforms such as Yelp or Amazon. Some platforms even tag their top tier of talent as "Top Rated." Recall from chapter 11 that Gigster used reputation scores they called "karma" to help decide who to staff on their projects. These reputation systems can cause substantial anxiety for workers who see it as singularly determining their fate;[2] in our interviews with Gigster workers, one referred to their karma score as "more important than money."[3] But we learned from workers at Gigster that when done well, the karma score can provide some sense of visibility and legitimacy to Gigster's staffing decisions.

A second individual objective is often cost. As any graduate of a neoliberal Economics 101 class will tell you, you are incentivized to keep your costs down when hiring. All things equal, you want to save money. Our experience is that lower cost typically means newer or less experienced: newer entrants to the market who are trying to build up a reputation often discount their services to make up for their lack of experience. You may have a positive experience working with them and find an amazing contributor who is early in their career, but it may also go poorly. It's tough to know up front. Workers with lots of experience, high ratings, and strong language skills in the clients' language tend to command the highest wages.

A third individual objective is availability: can this worker begin when you need them? Availability is one of the core characteristics that make flash teams unique: teams can be assembled very rapidly. But when you're ready to start, the highest-rated worker may already have a full schedule. Our flash teams approach uses an availability score as an estimate of how long we'd have to wait to get a response from the worker about an offer to join the flash team.

Team Objectives

Team objectives are the qualities of the team, rather than of individuals. Team objectives that can contribute to success include familiarity of team members with each other, diversity in team members, and the very practical issue of time zone overlap. These team objectives are often undervalued in traditional teams—but we have found that they are absolutely key in flash teams.

Although we might think that individual qualities such as higher IQ would lead to stronger team performance, research has indicated that in fact, group-level factors can be even more important to team success. Anita Woolley of Carnegie Mellon University and her colleagues ran in-person teams through a battery of different tasks trying to understand the key to teams with the strongest performance.[4] The average IQ of the team members and the smartest team member's IQ did not predict team performance. Instead, group interactions wound up being much more strongly predictive of the team's performance. So, the smartest teams are not just the teams of the strongest individual contributors!

One of the most useful team objectives is familiarity. In the flash teams world, workers are going to be convening with new teammates all the time. But, management researchers have observed a pattern in which a team's performance goes up the longer team members have worked together.[5] This is because people learn better how to coordinate with each other over time.

A second team objective is diversity. We are not the first ones to make the case for diversity in team composition and we will not be the last. Groups that integrate diverse perspectives produce better-performing solutions to challenging tasks.[6] As Scott Page of the University of Michigan has demonstrated through mathematical modeling, for many tasks, having a set of collaborators with diverse perspectives on a problem can outperform collaborators with more expertise, because the experts may be too clustered in one small subarea of the solution space.[7] One powerful thing about a flash team assembly engine is that it can build diversity directly as one of its objectives.

A third objective that we've found very practically useful is time zone overlap. Teams that never communicate with each other in real time can struggle to collaborate. So, this objective should put higher scores on teams that share at least, say, two working hours per day. Many workers publish their time zone availability on the platform, so this can be computed automatically.

Calculating team objectives can be done with a simple spreadsheet. It can more powerfully be done using AI too; we will go into that functionality next.

Using AI to Optimize Your Objectives

"Great," you may think, "you've given me a big pile of objectives. What the heck am I supposed to do with these?" Now it's time for AI to shine. If you give an AI your objectives and the ability to score each possible person and team by those objectives, it can dash off at superhuman speed to find the best solution.

But, you need to add one more piece of information, or else the algorithm is going to make Amelia Bedelia decisions. And that piece of information is how much weight the AI should place on each of your competing objectives. Why is it important that you tell the algorithm how to weigh its objectives? Imagine you hired a recruiter and told them that the ideal person you want is a graduating college senior with a good GPA in economics and some experience with financial forecasting software. Then the recruiter comes back to you: "There aren't any candidates who have both strong economics GPAs and financial forecasting software experience. Should I prioritize those with the GPAs, those with the experience, or give them equal weight?"

This is exactly the same kind of information you need to convey to the AI. There are all sorts of complex ways to do this, but the most common one—the kind of approach used by many tech companies—is to assign percentage weights to each objective. You want your main objective, for example, to carry 65 percent of the weight. If you care a lot about the reputation

Getting the Right Team in a Flash with AI Hiring

scores of the workers, you might set its weight at a healthy 20 percent. Likewise, if you are willing to give up on time zone overlap, you might decrease its weight to just 5 percent, or maybe even remove it entirely, 0 percent.

You'll want to experiment with these weights when you are first recruiting. Try testing some weights—for example, you might want the individual factors to account for 75 percent of the overall weight in the decision—and let your flash team software show you sample teams that it might recruit with those numbers. Look at why those teams are getting recruited—maybe it's because they are extremely highly rated, despite their cost—and adjust the numbers so that the results suit your needs.

Now it's time for the AI to do its job. We're not going to get into algorithmic details here, and in fact these algorithms are always improving. But just to give a high-level intuition of what the algorithm is doing: ideally, it would look at every single possible combination of workers into a team, and score that team. For example, if there were only three workers A, B, and C in the marketplace, and you wanted a team of two people, it would separately consider all possible combinations: A+B, B+C, and A+C. It then scores the objectives for each of those teams, weights the scores by the weights you gave it, and ranks the teams by those weighted scores.

In this ideal world, the algorithm checked out every possible combination of teams. But—and this is one of the classic problems in AI and computer science—checking every possible combination would take the algorithm a long, long time. With Upwork advertising 18 million active workers, there are over 971 quintillion possible teams of three people. If the AI had to check all of those combinations, you'd still be waiting long after you didn't need the team anymore.

So, the AI will find techniques that help it make these decisions quickly. One technique that we've used in our own work is to recruit the single best individual contributor for the project first, to anchor the team—for example, the worker with the highest reputation, or the role that will likely log the most hours on the project—and then add team members one by one afterwards based on who has accepted so far.[8] This is called a *greedy* algorithm because it always takes the best path immediately in front of it, never looking back to see if there was a better way.

Another technique we've used is to let the algorithm explore a few combinations that it finds initially promising, then backing out and trying other directions several times to gain confidence that its best known direction is

1. Identify your objectives		2. Weigh the objectives	3. AI finds combinations of people based on the weighted objectives	4. Team is recruited
Individual Objectives				
Reputation	4.9 stars	x10		
Cost	$30/hr	x2		
Availability	15% chance	x0.5		
Team Objectives				
Familiarity	10 projects together	x20		
Diversity	2/5	x5		
Timezone overlap	2 hours/day	x0.25		

Figure 12.1
AI can help with team staffing. Managers can experiment with the individual and team objectives they think are important, as well as the preferred weights of different objectives.

in fact better than any others it can find.[9] This is called a *stochastic search* because it's an exploration that rolls dice to occasionally rewind and restart—stochastic means "using randomness." Stochastic search, basically trying out lots of combinations and then looking around at slight tweaks on the options that seem promising, can work surprisingly well.

There is one last thing that you ought to know as a user of this AI software: your software is going to be dealing with declines and no-shows. There's no guarantee that the worker you want will accept the offer to join your team. Maybe they already have too many jobs; maybe you didn't offer a high enough salary; or maybe they're on vacation. So, not only does the assembly software need to identify the best team to match your objectives, it needs to do it without being sure that the people it identifies will say yes. Moreover, sometimes a worker will drop out after saying yes—for example, if they have an emergency.

The software needs to work despite uncertainty about who might actually accept the offer. One way to do this is for the software to keep a running guess as to the likelihood that each worker will accept your offer.[10] We multiply together the weighted score for that worker and the AI's estimated probability that they will accept the offer. So, if someone has a weighted score of 100 but there is only a 1-in-100 chance that they'll say yes, their value is 100*0.01=1.0; if another worker has a much lower score of 10 but a 50 percent chance of saying yes, their value is 10*.50=5.0. Through these value calculations, the software finds the workers who are both the strongest and most likely to accept your offer, so that you can recruit quickly.

Table 12.1

Possible Members of Two-Person Team	Individual Objectives		Team Objectives		Total Score
	Reputation 40% weight	Cost 30% weight	Team Familiarity 15% weight	Team Diversity 15% weight	Multiply each objective score by its weight, then sum them
Workers A and B	Worker A: 95 4.9 stars Worker B: 93 4.7 stars Team overall average reputation score: 94	Worker A: 35 $200/hr Worker B: 95 $50/hr Team overall average cost score: 65	50 *A and B have worked together for 30 hours on previous projects*	30 *A and B have highly overlapping professional networks*	94 * 40% weight + 65 * 30% weight + 50 * 15% weight + 30 * 15% weight = **69.1/100 team score**
Workers B and C	Worker B: 93 4.7 stars Worker C: 43 3.9 stars Team overall average reputation score: 68	Worker B: 95 $50/hr Worker C: 95 $50/hr Team overall average cost score: 95	0 *B and C have never worked together*	75 *B and C have largely non-overlapping professional networks*	68 * 40% weight + 95 * 30% weight + 0 * 15% weight + 75 * 15% weight = **67.0/100 team score**
Workers A and C	Worker A: 95 4.9 stars Worker C: 43 3.9 stars Team overall average reputation score: 69	Worker A: 35 $200/hr Worker C: 95 $50/hr Team overall average cost score: 65	100 *A and C have worked together for 1000 hours on previous projects*	10 *A and B have very highly overlapping professional networks*	69 * 40% weight + 65 * 30% weight + 100 * 15% weight + 10 * 15% weight = **63.6/100 team score**

By comparing different combinations of two workers—in this case a limited set of workers A, B, and C—the algorithm calculates scores for each objective, then weights them, to come up with an overall score for each team. Here, the team combining A and B wound up with the highest overall score.

Testing It Out: Team Assembly Experiments

Led by then–PhD student Niloufar Salehi, we demonstrated that flash teams assembly software can get the right people quickly. To do this, we brought in a crowd of over 200 workers from the Amazon Mechanical Turk online marketplace. Over a week and a half, these workers were convened repeatedly into different teams to write Google advertisements for Kickstarter projects. Since the teams were created at random times, workers were not always available—they might be eating, or sleeping, or taking a break, or doing other work.

Using our flash teams assembly software, we selected the factors of availability (likelihood that the worker would accept the offer quickly) and familiarity (team members' familiarity with each other as measured by the number of previous teams they had worked on together in the study) as the two main variables. The results were strikingly in favor of the power of the algorithmic hiring approach that combined both availability and familiarity to recruit and traded them off with each other via weights. Teams in this combined condition were far more likely to be able to actually convene a full team and finish the job. In fact, the teams in the combined condition successfully finished *twice as many* tasks as a control condition that used neither familiarity nor availability to recruit. We tried out other conditions, too, that used only availability or only familiarity—both of these helped, statistically speaking, but overall it was the combination of them that did the best. What's the lesson here? We need objectives, and not just a single objective: you will be most likely to recruit a full team if you combine the objectives and allow AI to make tradeoffs between them.

Did combined objectives lead to better performance? We actually went ahead and launched the Kickstarter product advertisements that the teams wrote on Google, which allowed us to measure click-through rates on the ads. Once again, objectives helped: teams that were hired using the familiarity objective had *double* the click-through rate of the control condition by the end of that study, reinforcing the power of objectives.

The workers themselves were much more enthusiastic about the more powerful assembly software conditions. When the software accounted for familiarity, two-thirds of workers appreciated working together with the same collaborators over time. As one told us, "We got into a groove and knew exactly what we were doing."[11] Another corroborated: "For my last

Getting the Right Team in a Flash with AI Hiring

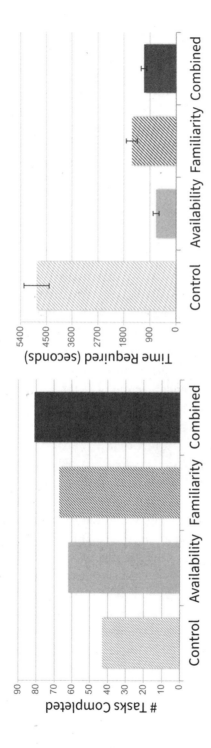

Figure 12.2
A recruitment system created flash teams whose membership optimized member availability, familiarity, or both.

couple of tasks as it was a quite familiar team by that point so we could relax and just have fun with the creative ideas."[12]

The control condition that didn't pay attention to availability or familiarity, in contrast, was a bit of a disaster: the software wasted between two and three offers on every team to workers who never responded or declined. As a result, it took the software roughly five times as long to finish recruiting entire teams in the control condition, so these workers faced long waiting times and about a one-in-six chance that their team would never actually finish getting recruited before the deadline. So, over time, the entire system unraveled, and workers became less and less likely to respond.

The Perils of AI-Driven Team Recruitment

There are reasons to believe, however, that the sort of AI team formation we've been discussing here might hit significant roadblocks. One reason is that people will almost certainly disagree with the algorithm's optimization of who ought to work with whom. For example, Diego Gómez-Zará and a team at Northwestern University observed that people ultimately wind up trying to shape team formation so that they can just work with their preexisting friends.[13] This ends up creating, in the researchers' words, "nondiverse and segregated teams, where most of the expertise and social capital are concentrated in a few teams." Ouch. A second reason is that people can be naturally skeptical of teams formed by an opaque algorithm. Farnaz Jahanbakhsh and colleagues at the University of Illinois found exactly this result when sorting people into teams—if the algorithm couldn't explain exactly why their teammates were chosen, they were unhappy.[14] Finally, a third potential roadblock, as observed by Emily Hastings and others at the University of Illinois, is that it can be very difficult to decide exactly which objectives to optimize.[15] How do you balance skill diversity against dispositional personality traits such as openness to experience and agreeableness, both of which are positively associated with better-performing teams?

To address these issues, you need to set strong public norms about what your team system is there to do. "We are looking for teams that bring together expertise, strong collaboration skills, and established track records," you might say. The exercise of setting your objectives and weights is ultimately a leadership one: what do you value, how much, and why? The issues above can arise if we don't decide on and then stand by our objectives.

What do we take away from all this? Thoughtful, human-centered AI can yield powerful flash team formation tools. Recruiting needs to balance several competing needs simultaneously; for example, the skill level of the worker, how soon they're available, and how well they work with other members of the team. In the past, hiring managers had to juggle these competing goals. However, drawing on algorithmic techniques from AI, we can craft algorithms that maximize team members' familiarity with each other even if we are uncertain about how available each person might be and are under strict recruiting time limits. The net effect is that you can get a team quickly that already knows how to work together. And you can rely on the software to do it—you don't need to be an expert in AI to reap these benefits.

13 Designing Flash Teams with AI in the Loop

You need to hire someone to create a mobile app that you brainstormed this weekend. You call a salesperson at Gigster and start to describe what you want. While on the phone with you, the salesperson starts checking the boxes in their standardized intake form to indicate the different features you want your app to have:

Settings page: check

Landing page: check

Photo upload: check

Needs to work on iPhone and Android: check check

All of these features are tags in their data collected from the many times Gigster teams have built apps for clients. They have a repository of source code and with the client's specifications, those feature tags help their system identify the source code that will be relevant for the new app. It also flags the specific skills that will be needed to complete it.

That sales call and the check-the-boxes template automatically deploys the source code and the structure of the team and recommends relevant experts. In a demo of these systems, Gigster puts the check-box form up on a screen right next to the window where another system is zeroing in on the starter source code for creating those features that the team can use.

As soon as the customer drops their credit card for the deposit at the end of the sales call, the system automatically starts a Slack channel as well as a GitHub repository with all of the relevant code from the host, structures the team roles, invites the team into the Slack channel, and off they go. The team members start collaborating immediately with all of the code and structures deployed based on those feature tags.

The flash team platforms that convene and support flash teams learn a lot about each team that they've seen: Who was on the team? What did they work on? How was the team structured, and how did they divide up their work? How closely did the team adhere to deadlines? What was the quality of the resulting deliverables?

Given enough of this data, AI can help you design teams that are likely to do well. These data enable you to ask: how can your flash team leverage the insights from every other team that has existed? Could it suggest the right number of people, the right kinds of expertise, and the right kinds of roles and division of responsibilities? Could it even help the team membership evolve over time?

You won't need a PhD in computer science for this. Trust us: one of us has one. What you will need, though, is data.

The Flash Team Library

To imagine what is possible, pretend for a moment that for every flash team in the world the following were fed into a global library of teams: a task list, a planned and completed workflow, original and changing role structure, chat transcript, milestone timestamp, video call recording, and deliverable repository. What would be in that library, and what could we learn from it? You could peruse the library looking for entries that look like the problems you're trying to solve. Maybe you could combine ideas from several of the entries. You could look at the margin notes from others who had previously checked out that entry, letting you know what worked well and what didn't. It would be like having all the institutional knowledge of every flash team at your fingertips.

How do we build this library, and how do we make sure that we (and AI) can make practical use of it? A library of teams could otherwise be a gigantic mess: if we didn't have an effective librarian and way of organizing, the whole thing could be a pile of stored files and notes lying on the floor. We have to find ways to organize the teams and help you and AI identify the elements that really matter. When we talked with Gigster cofounder Roger Dickey about how they learned to learn from flash teams data, we differentiated between "bottom-up" learning from the massive amounts of data produced by every flash team working on a digital system and "top down" interpretive structures that help you start to sort through.

Dickey used a metaphor around the flash teams DNA: "You have data on the people as a data object, the project as a data object, and the requested features. And you've got the tags that are able to coordinate all of those objects together." The Gigster HQ team was able to start by looking at all of the demand that their customers were bringing and tag the nature of the work the customers were hungry for.

He said, "We just pored over specs asking, 'What are common products of the day? What features are in Uber, Amazon, whatever . . . and you know, we're tagged about 120 common features that were about the same level of granularity." They were then able to map those tags back to teams, where relevant experts would get a text and a link giving them a chance to join a project as soon as the sales call ended that identified a feature with which they had experience and skill building.

Our team also developed a framing metaphor for a flash teams library. We thought about the different structures of flash teams as Lego blocks: those brightly colored blocks that children are obsessed with. Legos are simple shapes that can be combined into complex structures. Some Legos are simple, meant to be used everywhere. These come in shapes small and large, but they are the structural backbone of whatever you are building. Other Legos are unusual and oddly shaped, meant for very specific purposes.

Flash teams are made up of small Lego-like components, too. The most obviously visible block within each team is a task. Each task describes what someone is supposed to do, who is supposed to do it, how long it takes, what inputs it needs, and what outputs it produces. There are three blocks in the snippet of the flash team in figure 13.1: one that provides a usability evaluation of an interface mockup, a second one that takes that evaluation and the original mockup to produce a revised mockup, and a final one that takes the revised mockup and outputs a web application that realizes that mockup into functioning software.

What's useful about these blocks is that they are reusable—much as Gigster is reusing them when putting together a team to create an app for a client. Once anybody in the world has authored the usability feedback block and put it in the library, any other flash team can import it. The block contains all the information that's needed: what kind of person to hire, what inputs they should expect, and what outputs they should produce.

Like Lego blocks, flash team blocks can be combined into larger structures. The set of blocks above, which take in a user interface design, evaluate

Figure 13.1
Flash teams can be built as if from small, Lego-like components, with the main component being a task. Each task specifies what needs to be done, who will do it, the duration, required inputs, and expected outputs. A flash team might include tasks for evaluating a mockup, revising it, and coding a web prototype based on the revised mockup.

it, iterate on the design, and then produce a rough web implementation of it, can be reconfigured into lots of other combinations. For example, maybe the first two blocks can remain the same, but instead of a web prototype, you pass the mockup to a marketing team that can make a video showing off how the product might be used so you can gather customer feedback. Or maybe you can reapply the usability feedback block on the web prototype itself once it's built. The web prototype block itself is very general and you could apply it to many other teams, say, one working on a mobile website for your firm or one creating an announcement for an upcoming event.

Beyond task blocks, there is lots of other information that might be added to the library. For example, roles: every time you hire a person onto a flash team, the library might record an entry for that role. Maybe another flash team somewhere out in the world would need exactly that same role. Or maybe you need a role that someone else used before. Do you need a manager for a team of creatives? Check the library. Do you need someone with React Native development experience for social media applications? That role is in the library, too. Or perhaps you want a voiceover artist for a scientific-sounding video? Also there. As more people create flash teams, more and more of these roles, and guidelines for how to successfully hire for them, enter the flash teams library.

The library can contain hierarchies, too. How many people and what kinds of roles ought to be hired to make a YouTube advertisement for your project? If ten people are needed, should they be split into two smaller teams, or work in one flatter mega-team? The flash team library can contain examples of team hierarchies from all manner of deployments. Some organizations might have tried to keep them together; some might have split them up; some might have adjusted strategies midstream. The flash teams library will allow you to browse different ways that people organized their flash teams' hierarchy for tasks like yours.

You'll likely want one last piece of information in your flash team library in order to succeed: outcome measurements. How well did this team do? Were the workers happy? Stressed? Were they able to complete the task on time? How was the end product? Ideally, people contributing to the library use a combination of team feedback and performance feedback as the outcome. These outcomes can be critical for AI to be able to help, since we want the AI to focus on teams with good outcomes to the extent possible.

The flash team library can exist only if people feel comfortable sharing the data. Internally, many flash team companies such as Gigster and B12 create exactly this kind of internal library and history that they can draw on to templatize their own internal teams.

The two of us envision something more ambitious, a sort of public library of flash teams that anyone can access, more akin to Wikipedia. One approach is to make sharing with the library an exclusively opt-in decision. One possible future is a model inspired by the popular code repository GitHub, where many developers intentionally make their code open and visible to the world in hopes that others will use it and improve it.

In this framework, not a GitHub but a TeamHub, flash team experts are continually creating and publishing blocks and templates for others to use. Running a team would be as simple as clicking to download the blocks that fit your need, and then clicking "Go." A second futuristic model would aim to identify common patterns in a way that's anonymous. The structures of a successful flash team might start to seem like proprietary data. But we envision structures that do not "leak" information. Similar to how platforms such as Spotify analyze aggregate listening statistics in order to create playlists that match groups of peoples' tastes, TeamHub can create task blocks (like the one in figure 13.1) by aggregating statistics of how various people create those blocks. Another alternative is for a company to store the entire history of every flash team they run, but keep those data private to their organization. Your organization can bootstrap off of its own knowledge over time while keeping the record private.

Setting AI Loose on the Flash Teams Library

Leveraging a flash teams library, the future will see AI models that help you build a more effective team. You want to plan a marketing campaign for a new product? Here are the flash team designs that were the most successful at doing that, and an estimate of how much they cost. And based on prior marketing flash teams, here are the different ways that their hierarchies might look, how well the teams performed, and how happy we predict the teams to be under each of these hierarchies. This future is currently restricted to research labs and skunkworks prototypes, but it is coming.

Essentially, the goal of this kind of AI is to generate a team that matches your goals and performs well. One possibility is that the AI can help with prediction: what might happen if you launched this team, or that team? Suppose you described your goal in words, then the AI generated a team setup that is likely to be suitable for that goal. Based on prior runs of the team's blocks, roles, and hierarchy elsewhere in the library, the AI might then predict what might happen with the team. "Nice team you've got there—but since you're trying to build an entire mobile application, this team is likely to take four times as long as the current estimate. If you tried this other team structure, it'll cost more, but be done twice as fast." Or: "This team is very likely to turn in low-performing work without a project manager. If you add one, here's how it might affect cost and performance." Or: "We've seen a lot of teams try to do something like this. Ninety five percent of the time, they generally do well."

Suppose we know that the website development block from one team requires a user interface mockup as an input for them to implement. And suppose that a completely different team, one implementing a human-centered design process, produces a user interface mockup of a brainstormed design as its final step. By snapping these blocks together like Legos—by connecting the output of one team's design process block to the input of another team's website development block—we can create a team that never before existed, but does exactly what we need.

It turns out that searching and chaining blocks to blocks is something that AI is quite good at. So, you can tell the flash teams AI what you are trying to build, and the AI can search for and find the combinations of task blocks that will help you build it. The more teams are in the flash teams library, the more new combinations become possible. In the early 2000s,

Tom Malone and Kevin Crowston at MIT developed a handbook that categorized essentially every process that organizations follow.[1] If the flash teams library can encompass this broad set of processes, or manifest them in concrete team blocks, the flash teams AI could combine them toward a wide variety of goals.

What if all of this AI wizardry is just too risky for you? In that case, we suggest using one of the most mature and battle-tested AIs in the world: search. Search has been refined by academics and companies such as Google for decades at this point. (Yes, search uses AI algorithms.) What can search do to amplify flash teams? Well, when you've got a library, a good search engine can do a heck of a lot. In fact, the Stanford research project that gave rise to Google was called the Stanford Digital *Library* Project. When there are many thousands of flash teams in the flash teams library, search can help unearth the ones you are looking for. "I need a team of three to help me plan our Go To Market strategy for our product," you might think. Search for "GTM 3 people" in a flash teams search engine, and the search engine can return a list of all matching teams. You can grab what you like, edit it to customize it to your needs, and launch the team from there.

Ultimately, you'll have multiple options ranging from ambitious to fairly conservative. At the ambitious end, you'll be able to draw on AI to generate exactly the team you need based on pieces of previously known teams; you'll also be able to use AI to simulate how your team might go, and make changes in response. On the more conservative side, and in the shorter term, you can simply search through the library to find previous teams you've run that match your goals, edit them, and launch them. Or, even more pragmatically, your organization might curate a set of team templates that work well in your context, giving everyone a useful starting point.

14 Using AI to Improve Your Teams

Joanne's boss stops her in the hallway before the meeting: "I'm planning to ask you your thoughts on the roadmap, sound good?"

Looking into the conference room full of leaders mostly older than her, Joanne feels grateful that her boss is planning to signal the value of her opinion in a room that might not easily make space and recognize her as a junior team member.

Early in the meeting, her boss casually asks, "Joanne, what do you think?" and she's ready with an answer that helps the group understand some of the deep context that only she has, as the person driving the project. She continues to speak up and offer her expertise throughout the meeting.

Her boss had not always proactively helped make space for her voice during meetings. In fact, this move today was the result of him getting a "nudge" by text reminding him of his goal to help his team become more innovative through inclusivity. He had a calendar integration that reminded him that he had a junior person at his 11:00 a.m. meeting and that he intended to ask her thoughts early, because research showed that it's easier for someone to try speaking up in the first 10 minutes of the meeting.

We like this story where one manager gets a nudge to make one small adjustment in his own behavior in a way that amplifies the success of a junior team member and enhances the overall climate of his team. But what if we told you that this kind of one-off nudge is happening "at scale," as they say in Silicon Valley. That's workplace learning powered by AI.

In this chapter, we'll describe a few of these AI engines that facilitate team and organizational learning, including one that we prototyped. These systems all share a common structure that includes some data collection on how things are going, an intervention that is informed by that data, further data collection on how things are going after the intervention, and then likely another next intervention. These feedback loops are hard to get right, especially because they involve people and group dynamics, and because the systems builders are having to figure out how to collect useful data and design impactful interventions. But when they come online, these organizational learning systems can set up powerful feedback loops that represent organizations at their best.

In fact, if you think about it, that somewhat glib description of "see how things are going, make a decision based on that information, see how things are going, make a decision based on that information" is actually how organizations are assumed to work. Classic organizational theory says that information flows "up" from front-line workers and managers to leaders who then make targeted decisions based on that information that they send "down" the organizational chart to guide future behaviors. That classic image of an organization sees managers as primary decision-makers who use centralized information to identify problems and implement solutions.

These new AI-driven flash team HR learning systems similarly look to collect ongoing information so that managers can make targeted decisions intended to guide the organization to improved functioning. Of course, there are some clear differences between traditional organizations and these AI-driven systems, too. The feedback loops can involve more continuous engagement and can unfold at different levels of the organization. The systems can facilitate more immediate, distributed, and personalized behavior change, shifting the focus from top-down command and control to participatory, bottom-up organizational learning.

Perceptyx: Personalized Nudges at Scale with AI

The company behind the personalized nudges at the start of the chapter is called Perceptyx, and another standout story they like to tell highlights their platform's impact.

One of their customers is a $15 billion Fortune 500 company that is using Perceptyx's nudge system to drive behavior change at scale, with a focus on improving employee engagement, reducing attrition, and increasing productivity. They told us that traditional learning and development (L&D) systems do not scale effectively, and industry standard engagement rates for managers is around 7 percent. In strong contrast, this customer had an 83 percent engagement rate among employees, which obviously far exceeds traditional L&D benchmarks. The result was sustained habit formation over time, eventually translating into broader cultural and organizational transformation.

Joseph Freed, Chief Product Officer at Perceptyx, explained that, "The challenge a lot with L&D is you could either be personalized or you could be scalable. It's hard to be both. You can get a coach from Better Up—that's very personalized, but very hard to scale, right? Or you could be scalable, like LinkedIn Learning . . . or a license to Harvard Business Review. Well, that's not very personalized."

Their solution? Perceptyx created AI-powered "nudges," which are personalized, embedded in the flow of work, and aimed at steering managers and teams toward positive behavior change. The Perceptyx Activate AI Engine drives behavior change by:

1. Analyzing survey feedback and generating action plans
2. Sending personalized nudges to managers and teams to implement actions in daily work
3. Tailoring the nudges even more to individual roles as employees engage
4. Measuring engagement and impact across the organization.

The nudges address both individual- and team-level goals, and focus on research-based organizational interventions related to psychological safety and team performance.

The Activate AI Engine is a system offered by Perceptyx and is result of a seemingly elegant marriage between the following companies:

- **Perceptyx**, a company cofounded by John Borland in 2003 that had unparalleled success with employee voice through its comprehensive surveys and feedback systems. Perceptyx allows organizations to collect detailed employee insights across multiple touchpoints.
- **Cultivate**, a company cofounded by Joseph Freed in 2017 that developed a sophisticated personalization engine capable of generating AI-driven, context-specific recommendations for managers and employees, enabling behavior change in real-time and within the flow of work.
- **Humu**, a company founded by Laszlo Bock in 2017 and known for its extensive library of research-based nudges designed to promote positive workplace behaviors through small, actionable prompts tailored to different organizational roles.

These capabilities were developed by innovative teams in different companies and then unified when Perceptyx acquired Cultivate in 2022 and Humu in 2023. Together, these capabilities illustrate the power of AI folded into organizational learning. AI-driven systems, such as Perceptyx's Activate AI Engine, represent a transformative shift in how organizations facilitate learning, behavior change, and feedback loops, emphasizing continuous, participatory, and scalable organizational learning. These systems augment the traditional top-down, centralized decision-making model by enabling distributed, real-time feedback and personalized interventions at scale.

Bock, the founder of Humu, shared with us another case that illustrates the power of this approach. He was Senior Vice President of People Analytics at Google and is consistently introduced as "the closest thing the HR world has to a rock star."[1] Bock told us how Humu deployed its nudge system in a randomized control trial within a 5,000-person call center to boost employee productivity. The key focus was on improving factors like meaning and autonomy, which were identified as critical needs in the job. The nudges were personalized based on extensive performance data, even accounting for daily and hourly productivity variations. The results?

- Productivity increased by 8 percent, equivalent to moving from the 50th to the 98th percentile in performance—a significant impact given the limited range of performance variability in call centers.
- The system also smoothed out seasonal volatility in productivity, sustaining higher performance even during typically slow periods.

We learned that one common risk in these kinds of interventions is that managers can sometimes attribute these successes to their own management skills, even if there are clear, data-backed evidence for the system intervention. This risk can be a recurring challenge for AI-driven interventions.

Creating the Dream Team with AI

The Perceptyx AI engine has mostly been deployed in large enterprises, but by this far in the book, we know you see the potential for flash teams. Because flash teams' work is conducted entirely through online systems, you can use the data available to answer questions about how to structure *and restructure* your teams as the work progresses—including the roles, tasks, and hierarchies—through data and AI, not just relying on hunches. Should your team be flat or hierarchical? Friendly and collegial, or a bunch of call-it-like-it-is straight shooters? Should it make decisions collectively, or centralize decisions in a single member? Many such questions face every manager. They all roll up to the classic question: "What's the best way to organize a team?"

Unfortunately, research has shown that there isn't any single correct answer to this question—the best way to organize a team depends on who is managing it, who the team members are, and the task of the team. When we look at it this way, a lot of bad management decisions begin to make sense: managers start applying the correct solutions to the wrong team. Perhaps they use an organization that worked for them previously—but with a team that had a different goal. It's impossible to know *a priori* which approach is the right one for the team you're leading. It's a huge space to search for the right combination of decisions.

But, AI is *really* good at searching. So, Sharon Zhou of Stanford led a collaboration with the two of us to ask: can we leverage AI to help find the right way to manage a team?[2] The answer, as we will see, is yes. Imagine that, every so often, the flash teams software pings team members and either asks how things are going or looks at performance metrics. Based on the feedback, it suggests a change for the manager: "try a flatter hierarchy for a while," or "try round-robin conversations when there's a discussion or debate, instead of letting people talk freely." As the team tries these elements, this DreamTeam software, as we termed it, learns which combination works well for the team.

We can't simply throw AI at this problem and expect it to work. We have to design the AI to mesh well with how people work, or people are going to instead throw the AI out. Our goal here is to show you what that kind of human-centered AI looks like.[3]

To figure out the best set of structures for a team, the AI needs to try a bunch of different approaches. Under the hood, it does this by essentially running a bunch of different A/B tests on your team. You may have heard that the core AI technology underlying A/B tests is called a *multi-armed bandit*: it's an AI algorithm that estimates how well each option does, learning over time to throw more of its weight behind the options that seem to be performing well. And that's all well and good: we want the algorithm to be trying different options to sniff out what works for your team.

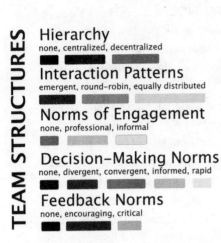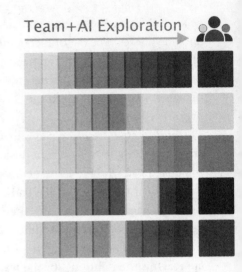

Figure 14.1
The AI-powered DreamTeam system helped teams adapt their structures over time. The system guided them to a combination of these team structures.

The issue is that each of the dimensions your team might depend on—hierarchy, norms of engagement, feedback norms, and so on—gets determined by a totally separate copy of the AI algorithm. That means that one AI might be changing your team's hierarchy to be flat and decentralized while another AI might be changing your feedback norms to be hypercritical and a third AI is telling you to suddenly ensure that everyone maintains equal speaking time. This is absolutely overwhelming. The mathematician would point out that, strictly speaking, this configuration is the theoretically optimal approach for the AI to identify the best settings efficiently. However, your team would revolt, which doesn't make it so optimal at all. So what do we do?

The first thing we need to do is teach the AI to respect human constraints. For example, people can only absorb so much change at once while they have a job to do. Luckily, research on teams can tell us more than that: it can tell us *when* a team is most open to changes in their working structure. And that time turns out to be closest to the midpoint of their project. If we were to draw this, it would look like an upside-down U shape with teams being the least open to changes at the start and end of the project, and the most open to changes near the middle.

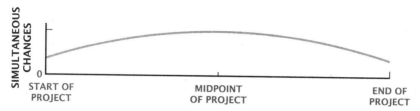

Figure 14.2
Prior research tells us that teams tend to be the most open to changes in their working structures closest to the project midpoint.

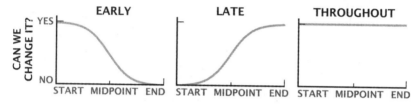

Figure 14.3
Prior research helped us consider the timing of changes. Research shows that some major changes to team decision-making should happen early, while changes to improve communication and coordination are best made during heavier execution phases. Some changes can plausibly be made at any time.

To do a better job, we ought to really also be paying attention to identifying a good or a bad time to make each change. Again the research literature has lots of help for us here: for example, some of the major changes to the decision-making structures of the team need to be figured out early, before the team ossifies into a less mutable way of getting things done. Other major changes are really most useful at the end, when the team is in heavy execution mode and more local changes to aid better communication and coordination are valuable. For a third category of changes, they are, in practice, equally changeable throughout the team's lifecycle: it doesn't really matter when they are changed. We can again draw this:

Now, all we need to do is make the AI respect these very human constraints and goals. Basically, we need to slow down the AI's explorations so that the teams can actually handle the changes, and make sure it's making the right changes at the right time. There's some fun math behind this. But essentially all you need to know is that we pump the brakes on the AI algorithms that are suggesting changes to the team. For one, we slow them all down in parallel so that they respect the first curve, with fewer changes at the start and end, and more in the middle. Then, second, we allow changes from the AIs that are a better fit for the current phase of the team—such as the start or end—and slow down changes from AIs that are responsible for other areas.

But does it work? Do AI-empowered flash teams do better? To test this, we divided 135 workers from Amazon Mechanical Turk into 35 teams. We gave the teams the ability to collaborate on Slack and tasked them with a series of ten challenging collaborative puzzles inspired by a difficult puzzle game called Codewords. Between each of the ten puzzles, the team might get advice from our AI algorithm about how to adapt their team. For example, they could opt to be a flat organization, or more hierarchical, or nicer to each other, or perhaps more cold and direct to each other. The AI needs a score in order to update its suggestions each round, so we used the team's score on that round's puzzle as its signal to determine how the team is doing.

Since this was an online experiment, not all teams got access to the AI. Some teams were given no direction at all, and figured out how to manage themselves. Other teams got all of the options that the AI had access to, and collectively decided each round what to try. Yet other teams appointed a manager, who made the decisions about what to try on their behalf.

The teams using our AI outperformed other conditions by 38 to 46 percent on average. In fact, the teams with AI were the *only* condition that outperformed the baseline teams that had no direction. But it wasn't just the existence of the AI that mattered. We also included an extra condition that used AI, but turned off the controls that we had enacted to slow down the AI's explorations. That is, the teams in this AI-enhanced condition were overwhelmed with so many options that they were unable to put any of them into practice. Those teams also did no better than the baseline. So the AI helped the teams—substantially!—but only when it was designed in a human-centered way to fit with how much change teams can really absorb.

Why did AI-augmented teams do better? One thing we observed from our data was that these teams simply explored more alternatives. Teams with human decision-makers, whether managers or collectives, fell prey to the classic problem of under-exploring: they tried a few alternatives, then effectively said, "Eh, seems good enough, let's stick with it." Likewise, in the condition where we gave the teams AI but didn't slow down its suggestions,

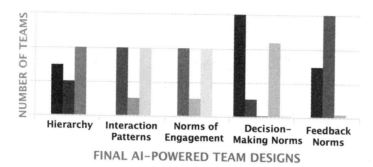

Figure 14.4
The AI-powered DreamTeam system helped teams experiment with many different team structures. In this study, teams did not converge on any one set of structures.

the amount of input was just overwhelming and the teams began to ignore it. The slowed-down AI was enough of a nudge for teams to get out of their comfort zones, but not so much that they started ignoring it.

Another benefit to working with the AI set at an optimal learning pace was that it helped each team find its own best combination of settings. When we looked at the combination of settings that each AI-augmented team wound up with, there was lots of variation: each team had found its own particular combination of traits that worked best for them. When the combination of possible options is this huge, then AI can be more effective at helping explore the options than we would typically be ourselves.

In fact, there's reason to believe that AI could do even better than this. The AIs in our study had absolutely no background information about which design combinations would work well for the teams. Using the flash team library, we can pre-train these AIs to have a general idea of what kinds of people and tasks tend to be a better fit for each design. With that in hand, you could imagine an AI taking your team into a one-hour kickoff session, trying on a bunch of different designs, and then launching your team preconfigured with a strong starter set of team designs.

Evolving Team Membership with AI

AI can also help you evolve your team *membership* in pursuit of more creative and innovative thinking. We explored this additional capability through a system developed by then–PhD student Niloufar Salehi of

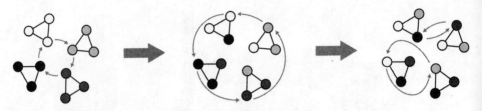

Figure 14.5
We created an AI system that assembled flash teams using network rotation.

Stanford. Ideas arise when old perspectives meet new perspectives—but in traditional teams, where we always work together with the same people, we sometimes miss out on those new perspectives. Salehi's idea was to create an AI system that allows people to work with a broader and more diverse network of collaborators over time.

It turns out that we can develop algorithms that weave collaboration networks over time—keeping the core of a team stable but slowly evolving team membership to connect new people to each other. We call this *network rotation*, where the collaboration network rotates members between teams over time.[4]

The AI here is relatively straightforward to describe: We want the AI to figure out, given the current collaboration network, who would be best to rotate onto which other team in order to preserve the core of the team but most usefully share ideas with your other teams. The implementation of our Network Rotation system, as we called it, is much less straightforward to describe: It involves asking the AI to try out many, many different combinations of moves and keep track of which ones might work best. Under the hood, for each possible move it might make, the AI needs to weigh how disruptive it is to the stability of the various teams against the potentially valuable outcomes in connecting disparate parts of the network.

In the figure below, we can visualize a collaboration network that might prioritize different outcomes for the teams. On the left, the algorithm only prioritizes team stability: people should keep working with the people that they know. So, all the lines stay between existing team members, keeping them stable. On the right, the algorithm only prioritizes connecting far-flung parts of the collaboration network. So, now the graph looks like spaghetti, which means that the teams rotated around so much that nearly everybody has worked with lots of different people, but nobody really got

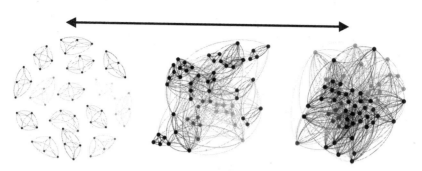

Figure 14.6
The AI-powered Network Rotation system produced statistically higher-rated proposals than the Stable teams and Connected teams conditions.

time to settle with their existing team. We might want something more like the middle graph, where the collaboration network does connect people across teams, but tries to keep teams stable too. As we discussed in chapter 12, algorithms like this one operate best when they're balancing multiple objectives rather than just aiming for one thing at the exclusion of everything else.

This network rotation approach works in practice. Our team collaborated with the tech nonprofit Mozilla, which is responsible for the Firefox web browser. Mozilla was interested in engaging their volunteer community in brainstorming better accessibility options for Firefox: how could the browsing experience be made better for people who are blind or have low vision, or have motor disabilities, or other disabilities?

Mozilla worked with us to organize the online design workshop, which attracted over a hundred disability experts, designers, and programmers. They formed these volunteers into small teams and wanted our network rotation algorithm to help diffuse the brainstorming conversations between teams. In tandem with our system, the participants brainstormed ideas ranging from interface elements that grow in size when you hold your finger over them on the phone to sign language gestures as inputs for the browser. They told us that the AI-based membership rotation brought some real benefits, if you were willing to deal with the slow trickle of team membership changes. One participant told us, "I liked bringing in fresh ideas every day. It gives a different/new perspective [. . .] but] sometimes you build good working relationships with others and do not want to lose them."[5]

The Mozilla deployment is useful in showing the real-world utility of this kind of approach, but it doesn't exactly prove that AI-based network rotation is better. To do that, we need the gold standard of social science: an experiment. We recruited 115 people off of the Amazon Mechanical Turk labor market, grouped them roughly into teams of four, and randomly assigned them to three conditions that mirror the three network graphs above. In a Stable Teams condition, the team stayed the same for the entire process. In a Connection condition, our algorithm moved people around to maximize the connectivity of the collaboration graph—lots of new connections made, but teams might be very disrupted. In the Network Rotation condition, our algorithm struck a balance between keeping teams stable and connecting the collaboration graph. We asked all the teams to brainstorm creative uses for a neighborhood common space. At the end of all of the phases of the study, we had a design expert code the quality of the resulting design proposals, without knowing which condition it arose from.

Compared to the proposals from the traditional Stable Teams condition, our AI-powered Network Rotation condition produced statistically higher-rated proposals—but the Connected condition, which gave the AI too much free rein over the social process, did not produce higher-rated proposals. In fact, the Network Rotation teams absolutely dominated the competition for the highest rated proposals, despite the expert not knowing which condition each proposal came from.

Why did this happen? Our thinking was that rotating the team membership would dislodge the teams from any brainstorming ruts they were stuck in. We definitely saw evidence of AI-powered membership rotation having the desired effect in the surveys we conducted of our study participants afterwards. Here's the kind of response we heard from someone in a control team, complaining that their group got too stale: "I didn't think this was a great team overall as our styles were too similar [. . .] I think new blood is sorely needed all around."[6] But for participants using AI-powered network rotation, they might convince their new teams to consider perspectives from their previous group, telling us: "I came up with a solution to a problem with one of the group's ideas. After that my contributions were taken into consideration [. . .] I came into a group with VERY different ideas than my original group."[7]

What do we take away from all of this? AI-powered team design tools can provide superpowers that even expert human managers might not otherwise have access to. So, if you manage a team using these AI tools, you can do far better than if you manage a team without these tools. But, you need to get very explicit about which objectives you care the most about. And you have to be careful not to overdo it: leaning too hard into the AI to the point that it disrupts your team will lead to a lot of effort and little benefit. If you find the right balance, AI can help you build exactly the team that you need, help you simulate how that team might succeed (or fail), help you find the right people for the team, and help you update team membership over time. All of this can lead to fewer coordination problems and more creative ideas.

15 AI for Flash Team Simulations

On February 13, in anticipation of Valentine's Day, Isabella spent time inviting guests, gathering materials, and enlisting help for a party at Hobbs Cafe. She convinced one of her friends, Maria, to help her decorate her cafe for the event. Maria had heard about the party from Ayesha, who had heard from Isabella. But Isabella didn't stop there: she told Sam about the party, who told Jennifer; she told Klaus, who told Abigail; she told Georgio, Eddy, John, Wolfgang, and Sam, too. All in all, twelve people all got word of the party.

Five came. Three people said they were busy—for example Rajiv, a painter, said "I'm focusing on my upcoming show, and I don't really have time." Four others said they were interested, but ultimately bailed out. Maria, who had been harboring a crush on Klaus, asked him to join her at the party, which he accepted.

This chain of events would be unremarkable for a small town. But it is far more remarkable for us: every single "person" above was actually an AI agent. They independently planned, coordinated, and showed up to a party in a simulated environment *without any user direction*. These are not the party plans of people or even the human users in a simulated game. Isabella Rodriguez is a generative AI agent powered by a large language model and some additional architecture developed by Joon Park and Bernstein as part of a team of faculty and researchers at Stanford and Google. Information about this party diffused autonomously during the simulation.

Notice that one feature of the AI agents in the simulation is that they were coded with *roles*. What could we learn about flash teams using role-based simulations?

AI for Team Simulations

What if AI could simulate a test run of your team and your planned role structure before you actually launch it? You're probably familiar with simple simulations, like the massively popular game *The Sims*, where computer characters live their lives in an interactive dollhouse and town that you control. Park, Bernstein, and team took this idea to the next level, using large language models such as ChatGPT to create believable simulations of human behavior.[1] We gave these AI agents the ability to talk to each other, to remember their previous experiences and their previous interactions with each other, and to analyze their experiences to form higher-level reflections. These *generative agents*, as we called them, were viewed by human evaluators as engaging in extremely believable behavior. We had created AI proxies that could act much like people do.

We went so far as to create a small town of AI agents, which we creatively named "Smallville," and allowed those agents to live out their simulated lives in Smallville so we could observe their social dynamics. Agents engaged in all sorts of activities: college students went to school, shopkeepers attended to their stores, and generally agents got to know each other. All in all, it felt like a plausible simulation of human behavior.

Again, notice that these agents are assigned roles and personas and use those understandings to guide their behavior and interactions. Here's how it worked:[2]

> "To directly command one of the agents, the user takes on the persona of the agent's "inner voice"—this makes the agent more likely to treat the statement as a directive. For instance, when told "You are going to run against Sam in the upcoming election" by a user as John's inner voice, John decides to run in the election and shares his candidacy with his wife and son."

The agent John now understands his role as mayoral candidate and uses that understanding in future interactions. The human user can also use natural language to communicate roles by telling an agent the role that the human user is acting within, so that the agent knows how to interact with them:[3]

> "If the user specifies that they are a news "reporter" and asks about the upcoming election by saying, "Who is running for office?", the John-agent replies: My friends Yuriko, Tom and I have been talking about the upcoming election and discussing the candidate Sam Moore. We have all agreed to vote for him because we like his platform."

AI for Flash Team Simulations

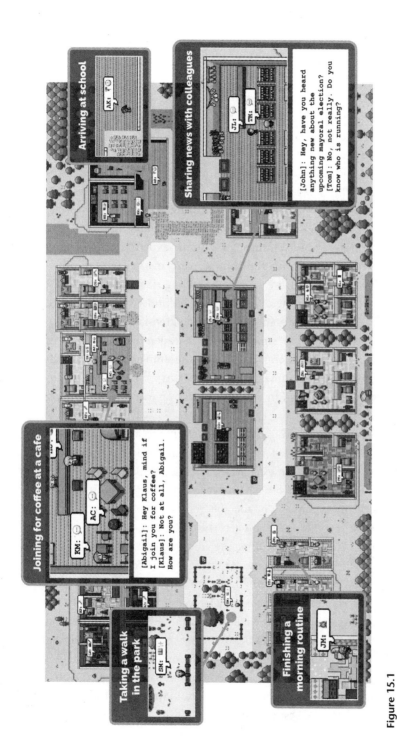

Figure 15.1
We used modern large language models to simulate human behavior. We coded AI agents that could talk to each other, remember past interactions, and reflect on their experiences. Human evaluators found their behavior highly believable.

This interaction "works" because both parties have an understanding of the role structure and what that means for their expected knowledge and behaviors.

Building on the work of generative agents, we can envision using these AI-powered simulations to design and test flash teams in dynamic, role-based environments. Imagine creating a simulation populated with agents assigned to specific roles like UI designer, UX designer, front-end developer, back-end developer, and QA specialist. By running these agents through hypothetical flash teams projects, we could test different team configurations and workflows—for example, comparing how a team performs with and without a project manager. This approach could highlight potential bottlenecks, miscommunications, or gaps in expertise, offering insights into how to structure teams for optimal performance. Importantly, these simulations could be run repeatedly, providing not just a snapshot but a probabilistic understanding of likely outcomes under varying scenarios.

This kind of simulation can help bring up potential failure modes. When we evaluated these kinds of simulations with leaders of online communities such as Reddit subreddits, the leaders used the simulation results to change their community rules before any of the negative things they saw in their simulation ever happened in real life. It's like an early warning system for interpersonal drama.

Going even further, why run the simulation only once? The great thing about simulations is that if we can run them once, we can run them a hundred or a thousand times. This lets us understand: what are the more likely, and less likely, outcomes? Do things go smoothly most of the time, and occasionally slip up in a predictable way? Or do they usually crash and burn, and is it rare that this team gets things done on time?

Of course, AI simulations of people are not the same as real people. So the AI can—and will—be wrong. It's entirely possible that the underlying large language model behind the AI might have some blind spots, so that its simulated people may categorically be too nice or too mean. In fact, we know that this can be the case already, from our own work on these simulations. Those kinds of errors can be somewhat corrected for, but the real risk is the error that we *don't* know about yet. So don't bet your life savings on the outcome being exactly the same as the simulation predicts. But, these kinds of AI simulations can help us understand what might occur, and take steps to design for the best outcome.

Training Interpersonal Skills through AI Simulation

Speaking of AI simulations, can AI help your flash teams learn to work better together? Better collaboration means a better experience and better outcomes. Few of us get effective training on how to play well with others. These abilities are often devalued as "soft skills." But devaluing these skills couldn't be a worse idea. In reality, interaction skills have a substantial influence on team performance. Science has documented this well—you can look up the citations. (We did.[4]) But you can probably prove it to yourself by reflecting on the last team you were on that had a real jerk in it.[5] It didn't matter how skilled everyone was—the team probably flailed and underperformed.

This section lays out the horizon of how AI can offer simulations for flash teams in order to train them and provide practice on skills that matter. Interpersonal skills are tough to train. Of course, you can read a book about it. Unfortunately, that's not enough. Learning a new skill requires what educational researchers call *deliberate practice*: you need to try a skill, get immediate feedback, and then iterate and try again.[6] Practice your new tennis shot, get feedback from your coach, then try the shot again, and again, and again. How are you supposed to get practice at difficult interpersonal skills like managing conflict without practicing on—and summarily pissing off—all your colleagues?

AI provides remarkable opportunities here. Omar Shaikh, along with Diyi Yang, both at Stanford, collaborated with Bernstein to develop an AI rehearsal platform for exactly these kinds of situations.[7] We are able to construct simulated people with whom you can practice conflicts. What do you do when one of your reports isn't responding to feedback, for example? We can create simulated people, and let you rehearse different responses and see what happens.

Creating an AI that can mediate conflicts in realistic ways isn't as simple as flipping a switch. Initially, when we introduced ChatGPT into simulated conflict scenarios, it either played the role of a stubborn enforcer or caved way too quickly. We knew there had to be a way to inject more sophistication, but AI alone wasn't going to get us there.

Enter Michele Gelfand. The timing was perfect; Stanford's Graduate School of Business had just brought her on board as a negotiation expert, and she introduced us to a powerful concept: the Interests–Rights–Power framework.[8] This model maps out the main strategies people use in conflicts.

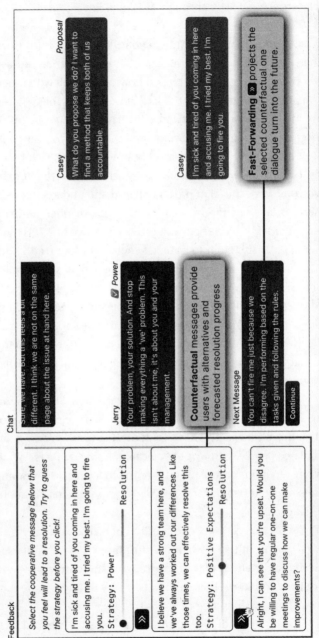

Figure 15.2
We integrated the Interests–Rights–Power framework into our AI. In an experiment, participants who practiced with our AI system used fewer competitive strategies and more cooperative ones, managing conflicts significantly better than those who didn't use the AI training.

◀────────────────────────────────

Interest-based strategies focus on aligning with the other person's goals, *rights*-based appeals rely on shared norms, and *power*-based strategies involve force or coercion. What was intriguing—and highly relevant for training AI—was that each approach leads to very different outcomes. For example, relying on power tactics like threats can quickly escalate a conflict.

We saw an opportunity to hybridize our AI with this framework, giving it the ability to predict likely responses based on the strategies people use. Now, ChatGPT wasn't just responding—it was thinking about why someone might react a certain way. Picture this: you propose a course of action, and the AI says, "Hmm . . . that sounds like a rights-based approach. Are you comfortable with that? Here are two ways the other person might respond." This layer of self-reflection turned ChatGPT into a more thoughtful sparring partner and gave users real-time insight into how their choices could escalate or de-escalate a situation.

To see how well this hybrid model worked, we ran an experiment. We brought forty people into the lab, gave everyone an overview of the Interests–Rights–Power framework, and then split them into two groups. One group used our AI rehearsal tool to practice conflict scenarios with simulated personas; the other group received no such practice. After training, both groups engaged in a live text-based conflict with one of our graduate students, who had no idea which participants had received the extra training.

The results? Remarkable. Although both groups knew the theory, the group that practiced with our AI managed conflicts more smoothly and cooperatively. Manual analysis of their conversations showed that they used de-escalating, interest-based strategies twice as often, and power-based, competitive strategies one-third as often. In short, practicing with our AI didn't just teach the framework; it turned it into second nature.

Together these two studies envision a future in which AI simulations can help teams design, evaluate, and even troubleshoot interpersonal dynamics before they play out in the real world, offering a powerful tool for building stronger, more cohesive teams.

16 Predicting Flash Team Outcomes with AI

A group of five remote workers is collaborating on a fast-paced web ad project. They're just getting started: they've been brought together through a flash team platform, with a clear deadline to produce compelling Kickstarter ads by Friday. On the surface, things seem to be going well: everyone logs in, greets each other, and starts generating ideas. But beneath the pleasantries, an AI system monitoring the team's interactions flags a potential issue.

A pattern has emerged that the AI has seen before: one team member, Olivia, is talking a lot and using a bunch of language focused on her ideas and opinions. Meanwhile, Nathan is responding to ideas with skepticism—phrases like "yes, but . . ." and "are you sure about that?" This kind of conversational dynamic is correlated with a high risk that the team will get into conflict and fracture in the long term, even if the team continues to perform well in the short term. Olivia's self-centered focus and Nathan's passive criticism are a ticking time bomb.

The AI system predicts that the team has an 85 percent chance of experiencing interpersonal conflict before the project ends. It sends a private message to Lucy, the team's manager—"Potential fracture detected"—and links to examples of the behavior and what the resulting risk might be. It continues: "Consider an open team discussion and check-in to encourage more inclusive dialogue."

Lucy, aware of the fast-moving nature of flash teams, initiates a casual video call. She looks to build a more cooperative team dynamic by encouraging collective planning and constructive feedback.

We've all had the experience of being on a team and just *knowing* that the team is skating on thin ice. Something feels off about the team's vibe: people are a bit out of sync, they're talking past each other in ways that aren't immediately causing problems but are likely to escalate later, or you can just feel in your bones that someone is not a good fit for this team. As instructors of team-based project classes, the two of us regularly see teams that simply cannot wait for the end of the term so that they never have to talk to their teammates again. Sometimes those teams are poor performers; sometimes the teams perform well together but can't wait to be rid of each other: "Thanks, nice to work with you, I hope I never have to do that again."

Wouldn't it be nice if AI could help flag potentially upcoming team issues, so that they could be addressed before they flare up and irrevocably break trust among team members? In a future of flash teams, this becomes far more possible than it is today. Could AI help you pick up on indirect signals that might signal future escalation? Are team members talking in ways that suggest they may not be on the same page? Are some members being silenced or railroaded into submission?

Predicting a Team Disaster with AI

Researchers John and Julie Gottman can predict which couples would eventually divorce just by watching them have a conversation about a topic of marital disagreement for fifteen minutes. By scoring those short conversations for how often the couples were criticizing each other, saying "yes, but...", getting defensive, putting each other down, and engaging in other behaviors, the researchers could predict with 83 percent accuracy which couples would divorce within ten years.[1]

Malte Jung of Cornell University led a study following this model but focused on teams rather than marriages. After observing fifteen minutes of a team's interactions, Jung's team manually coded how positive or negative the team's language was when members spoke to each other, and how often team members engaged in specifically hostile behaviors. And just as in the original divorce study, Jung and his team were able to predict, up to six months in advance, with 91 percent accuracy, whether a team would be high- or low-performing.[2]

Our research team at Stanford took the next leap: we built a team early-warning system with AI. We had remote teams engage in a collaborative task of creating web ads for Kickstarter projects using group chat software.[3] Each person worked with several different teams on these tasks. After they

Predicting Flash Team Outcomes with AI

worked with each team, every member of the team privately filled out a survey responding to questions about whether the team was cohesive or falling apart and whether the team was able to address problems; they were also asked whether the team should continue working together in the future.[4] Averaging these survey results across team members gives us an overall score for each team. Let's call this a *team fracture score*: the likelihood that the team members want to break up. In addition to the team fracture score, we also measured the performance of those teams by launching their Kickstarter ads and measuring click-through rates.

Together with Hancheng Cao and Mark Whiting of Stanford, we trained an AI algorithm on this dataset to automatically predict each team's fracture score. In order to predict that fracture score, the AI was only able to use the publicly visible information contained in the text of the group chat software that the team used to communicate as they did the task. The algorithm honed in on expressions of disappointment, as well as the presence of highly polarized team members who are either extremely peppy or extremely grouchy. It also compared the use of "me" language (e.g., "I", "me", "mine") vs. "us" language (e.g., "we", "us", "our"). With this data, the algorithm of the AI was able to identify teams at highest risk of fracturing with 88 percent accuracy. It turns out that it's even easier to identify the teams that are doing well and are at the least risk: our algorithm achieved this at an even higher 92 percent accuracy.

How far can we push this? The original studies on married couples used only 15-minute slices of interaction. How little of a glimpse of a team's interaction do we really need for our AI algorithm to work? We started winding back the clock on our algorithm, giving access to smaller and smaller windows of time at the start of the team's conversations. What if we gave it access only to the first half of the team's interaction? The first third?

The AI algorithm needs very little interaction data to make its prediction, it turns out. To identify the teams at highest risk of fracturing, the algorithm needed only the first three minutes of the team's interactions. In other words, the algorithm performs nearly as well with just three minutes of data as it does with the full ten minutes of data. To identify the best teams—those at the lowest risk of fracturing—the algorithm only required the first *70 seconds* of team interaction.

Imagine what you could do with this kind of AI. If you're a manager of a team, you might get an early-warning signal that something is not working with your team. You could then intervene: look carefully to figure out what's likely causing the issue, talk to the impacted team members, and make plans for a remedy. If you are the one causing the issue, maybe you'd get a quick private heads-up, or maybe your manager gets the quick nod and can work with you privately on it.

These AI predictions are fallible, and any good manager will keep this in mind. They are predictions, not magical insights into the future. Maybe the algorithm is thrown off by a peculiarity in how your team is interacting. Maybe your team is just near the threshold, but the algorithm has to make a call one way or another, and the team is slightly more likely to be at risk than not, so it's classified as at-risk even though there are still decent odds that the team could pull it out on its own. Maybe getting flagged as at-risk could actually nudge the team in a way that makes it spiral worse—it would have avoided the issue before, but naming it lights the fuse. It's important that these tools be seen as augmentations, not automations, so that the very real people who are impacted by them have autonomy and can make well-informed decisions.

Launching the Best Version of Your Team

Mark Whiting found a way to combine all of these insights into a clever team launching strategy that helps flash teams start off on the right foot—and stay there.[5]

Because so much about a team experience depends on early interactions—seemingly small and inconsequential behaviors will cascade into success or fracture—we wanted to give teams a chance to shake off any bad luck and capitalize on effective starts. To do this, we created a flash team incubator platform. We took the insight behind our team fracture project to its logical conclusion: imagine if you really could turn back the clock on a ruined team. Lacking a Delorean, going back in time seems like a flight of fancy. But, through clever technology, we can convince people that's exactly what has happened.

Imagine that you're a new flash team member engaged in an online interaction. When you arrive, our incubator platform gives you a random pseudonym: "Charlie-O," "Sally-P," or something along those lines. You, Charlie-O, work together with your team for a bit. The platform tells you that it's now time to try out another team, and you're randomized into another group. So you, as Charlie-O, work with this second team, then a third team. Finally, the incubator says that you're getting reconvened with the team that collaborated together most effectively, you drop the Charlie-O pseudonym, and your team launches.

The trick is you did not interact with three different teams during these three rounds. You were in fact working with the exact same people the whole time, their identities had just been masked by the platform. While it looked to you like you had the same pseudonym Charlie-O the whole time, to everyone else you looked like a completely new person because you had a different pseudonym each round: instead of Charlie-O, you might have appeared to others in one round as Steve-O, and in another round as Bobby-O. Our incubator platform intercepted all messages mentioning Steve-O or Bobby-O and rewrote them so that, to you, they looked like your original nickname, Charlie-O.

In effect, you perceived yourself to be working with a different team each round, but it was the same people—just anonymized and restarted. We surveyed the teams at the end of each round to identify the round that was most preferred and then told people they were working again with that preferred team for a final round. We tested this incubator launchpad in an experiment with 143 participants from Amazon Mechanical Turk.

When a team thought they were working with the team from their most preferred round, rather than an entirely new team, their likelihood of wanting to work together again went up by five-sixths of a standard deviation: a large effect. But, keep in mind, because of experimental design, they were always working with the same group of people each round. (By the way, we tested our participants to see if they could figure out who was who in their original teams—and almost nobody could.)

This result shows that by anonymizing team members and resetting their interactions, the platform gave teams a "fresh start," suggesting that reframing or restarting interactions can help groups mitigate early missteps. It wasn't about the specific individuals being inviable as a group, it was about how their interactions got them off to a rough start. Indeed, the experiment highlights how initial team interactions strongly influence how team members perceive the "quality" of their collaboration. If participants believed they were reconvening with their best-performing team, they were significantly more likely to want to work together again—but, again, it was the same group the whole time. Leaders can potentially salvage fractured teams and create conditions for stronger collaboration, even in cases where early interactions seem to doom the group to failure. This insight may be particularly valuable in flash teams or other temporary online groups.

This entire pipeline leverages opportunities that would be difficult to implement with traditional teams but are straightforward for flash teams. We've seen in this section how AI should be able to train teams in interpersonal skills, predict with a high degree of accuracy which teams will be successful and which will fail, and help launch those teams with a greater chance of success. Because much of flash teams' interactions happen online, AI offers possibilities for helping managers monitor teams. AI can continuously (and privately) run analytics on the text chats and video meeting transcripts, then reach out if there are early warning signs that the team might run into issues. Then, because the team members are convened online, an incubator platform can try out several configurations—even if those configurations are exactly the same people, just masked from each other—and launch the team when it has hit its stride.

AI Predictors of Other Flash Team Outcomes

We'll tell you about one final study that illustrates how AI can predict team outcomes. This result was led by then-PhD student Katharina Lix based on data from over a hundred Gigster teams that she analyzed for her dissertation.[6] She analyzed the entire chat transcripts of teams talking to each other on Slack using AI to explore how flash teams talk to each other.

The remote, on-demand teams varied considerably in how similar team members' language was to each other. In some teams, their words and phrases were very similar to each other, and for other teams, the words and phrases each team member used were more diverse. You might expect such differences within teams, but it's interesting to show that the convergent or divergent language patterns mattered to their success. Because these differences indeed predicted the teams' performance.

During ideation tasks—like brainstorming sessions—the teams benefited from high levels of divergent language, where varied interpretations and novel ideas can lead to innovative solutions. Conversely, during coordination tasks, divergent language hindered performance, as alignment and clear communication are more critical. In one case, a team engaged in the planning phase of a software sprint initially showed very convergent language to align on goals. However, during daily troubleshooting and brainstorming sessions, the language shifted and diverged as team members explored multiple solutions. Lix's innovative study, which advanced the state-of-the-art of natural language processing at the time, shows how even teams' working chat channels can offer a lens for seeing how well members are coordinating with each other.

As a leader, you're likely familiar with the challenges of team dynamics—how a promising start can turn turbulent, or how a high-performing team can unexpectedly lose its spark. The insights presented here should empower you to take advantage of AI's predictive capabilities to understand your teams in real-time, flag potential issues early, and build stronger, more cohesive groups. AI doesn't replace your judgment or intuition; instead, it offers a new lens for spotting potential fractures before they widen into conflicts and for identifying collaboration patterns that signal thriving teamwork.

17 Building a Healthy Ecosystem for Flash Teams

Things change when you become a parent. The hours you kept before you had kids no longer seem feasible. You start to see that you're trading off between some of the truest parts of yourself—one part who wants to be there for these chubby-cheeked kids who you love more than life and the parts of you who want to grind and work and solve problems at the highest level, having real impact in the world.

For Catalant cofounder Rob Biederman, dissolving that trade-off is one of his proudest accomplishments in creating Catalant. He believes that their on-demand, remote, AI-enhanced team business model keeps women, parents, and others who get pushed out by rigid in-person schedules more engaged in the workforce.

But he thinks to get to this "philosophical unlock," clients had to believe and realize that freelance talent would be capable of producing the same or better outcomes as the traditional consulting firms. Catalant was able to build to that paradigm shift because it can offer to talented, experienced experts the kind of "work that fits neatly into the life they'd imagined and work they can do at the highest level."

Biederman told us, "This wasn't busy work, and it wasn't kind of check-the-box stuff. This is serious consulting for boards of Fortune 100 companies that informs strategic decisions on a billion-dollar scale. In fact, there was one business that somebody started and then sold for the better part of $100 million largely with revenue that they sourced on our platform."

Imagine yourself in ten years. You wake up, turn on your laptop from your home or shared physical coworking space, and log in to work. The work platform recalls your skills and abilities (say, video production), then matches you immediately to a team of other experts around the world.

The system tells today's team that a client wants help putting together a marketing plan for a new product. You've never met your teammates, but they all have stellar reputations, so you jump in using videoconferencing, a shared folder, and an online team room. A week later, the platform has connected you with a different team to collaborate on a documentary. As your career advances, a year later, you've joined a digital organization that has hundreds of people but no physical headquarters—one that brings in people with new skills as needed to navigate the marketplace.

For years, your computer has been a tool for getting work done. When work arrived from your manager or colleague, you sat down to a blinking cursor and used your computer to write the report, or create the spreadsheet, or send the email. Work arose from the in-person world. It got done on the computer.

That relationship, happy or unhappy as it was, is giving way to one that's far more transformational. The computer no longer is just our tool for doing work: it is becoming an instrument that gives us work. Online, networked societies have embarked on a massive shift to take work online. Already, marketing professionals, programmers, house cleaners, administrative assistants, performers, and more are available on-demand and are made accessible by algorithms and applications. This change signals a shift to complex, interdependent work at scale on the Web. The computer is its mediator and its enabler.

We have been spending our time discussing how to create and manage flash teams, but the entire foundation of our economy has already shifted. If you buy our basic premise—experts everywhere, all the time—then you already know that work has become digital and networked. Any work now done at a computer could be done remotely by members of "the crowd." Economists have estimated that about 20 percent of US jobs could be outsourced, to the tune of 45 million full-time jobs, and a large percentage of those could happen through the kinds of online platforms we have discussed in this book.[1] What began with outsourcing, and then paid crowdsourcing and gig work, is now likely coming for white-collar desk jobs.

Catalant creates flash teams from their network of business professionals with great success. Similarly, the company A.Team creates flash teams from their curated network of tech professionals. A.Team founder and CEO Raphael Ouzan said that, even though they started in stealth mode, they could not keep up with demand to join their network. He told us, "However highly curated it is and however hard we made it to get into, we kept getting so many applications, so many people that wanted to be a part of it. We had product management, Android designers, engineers, data scientists, from big tech firms and startups alike."

Yet, even as this sector grows, we need not look too far to understand growing concerns about why this kind of digital work could be a bad thing. Uber drivers are suing and organizing for better representation.[2] Workers on the Mechanical Turk platform have seen their income stream cut off by changes in platform policies or capricious requesters who reject their work for no discernable reason. Mary Gray and Sid Suri have documented this shift thoroughly in their book *Ghost Work*.[3] What does it mean when your administrative job, or your mid-level management job, or your programming job becomes subject to more algorithmic management? If a poorly designed algorithm is telling you who to work for, or how well you did, or how much you earn, what negative impacts will that have on your life and job satisfaction?

It's time to consider what we can do to prevent these negative outcomes. Can we build a future of work that we want to live in—quickly enough—to see it avert the future that we don't want to live in?[4]

Finding Our North Star

We can learn from the known problems in the gig economy, which often involve remote work and algorithmic management. We'll list the specific issues next, but let's start with the big picture: gig work disrupts an assumed social contract between workers, employers, and government. Workers provide labor, employers provide money, and the government makes sure everyone follows the rules. This social contract was codified in the industrial revolution. In more recent times—say, the past hundred years—employers also provided various types of support for their workers. These might include health care benefits, retirement or pension savings, guaranteed wages, structured paths for career growth, and workplace safety standards. With a future of online work, we are splitting work apart from these pillars of support. You can work flexibly when and where you want, yes, but you no longer have a stable income in between jobs, health or retirement benefits, paid time off (PTO) in the form of sick days or vacation days, or structured career growth opportunities.

Some leaders, such as Natalie Foster of the Economic Security Project, suggest we should reverse this: government provide the benefits and protections to workers, while companies pay wages and contribute more to the overall pot. Foster's book, *The Guarantee*, argues for expanding the economic floor in America to include guaranteed housing, health care, family care, higher education, good work, income and an inheritance. This kind of proposal offers a north star in social policy that protects workers and gives people the stability needed for flexibility to be felt.

"It's *trampoline capitalism*," Foster explained when we asked her how a guaranteed economic floor would impact flexible workers. "When people have economic stability, they take more risks, can pursue a college degree or start a business. They're more entrepreneurial. And we have a natural experiment to point to: when people had more money in their pockets during the COVID-era policies of the 2020's. By 2023, we saw small business creation go up by 59%, the first time we'd seen that in decades. Investing in the American people would unleash creativity and ingenuity."

Building from this vision, what can we do about the problems that seem inherent in gig work? Maybe we could define our goal as reversing the trends listed below. But this feels incomplete: are we just throwing a patch on a broken pipe, so it's going to just break again in different ways? Could we identify a North Star goal that animates us more effectively?

Here is one vision for that goal: Can we create opportunities that workers *prefer* to equivalent traditional work, instead of platforms that workers turn to only when their traditional work falls through? What would it take to create an online work ecosystem that is a clear and desirable way to build a career? What would it take to motivate the most skilled workers in the world to aim for jobs online? In their marketing, today's platforms boast a value proposition of schedule flexibility, independence, and work-life balance, but those are clearly not yet enough to create sufficient incentives for many skilled workers. You may personally know a few early adopters who already make their skills available on online work platforms, but for many, a traditional employment contract is still the preferred option.

That North Star directly orients us toward addressing the risks that an online worker faces. Even if workers find jobs, they need to immediately begin lining up for the next one. Add to that the fact that there are no paid sick days or PTO or health care benefits for online platform workers. For most workers, the risk of a dry spell with no work and no income is

Building a Healthy Ecosystem for Flash Teams

frightening. We're hardwired to minimize risks, and in this case, it seems rational that we do so. What would it take to make joining the online workforce not feel like such a risk?

The Potential Harms in Online Gig Work

At present, many known problems face workers engaged in the online gig economy. These are useful to understand when considering a health ecosystem for flash teams and the changes needed to make it an economy where everyone can thrive.

Wage Theft

One major concern for expert contract workers has been wage theft. Wage theft occurs when you complete your work but your employer doesn't pay you for it. Imagine that you spent two weeks on a project, sprinting to meet a deadline. Your personal life takes a hit—you're temporarily sidelining your social life, exercise, and maybe even some sleep time to get this done. But you complete the job; you made it! Then, the client takes weeks to take a look, and eventually decides it's not what they were looking for. They want you to revise your work on a tight schedule before paying you. Or they want you to revise your work without any additional payment for your time. Or, even worse, they flat-out refuse to pay you. You're out of the income while this gets resolved—if it ever does get resolved. And while the platforms often take ownership of identifying and removing bad workers, they are not particularly incentivized to go after and remove paying clients even if they are misbehaving.

Getting Started

Another challenge for contract workers is the sheer difficulty of getting your first jobs in a global labor market. It's the classic Catch-22 of getting your first job: How do you convince someone to hire you when you have no prior experience, but how do you get that experience when nobody will hire you without it? When Bernstein was younger, he wanted to make video games for a living. When he applied for those jobs, the question he'd get from the big video game companies was, essentially, "So why haven't you been making games already?" Bernstein, frustrated at the time, thought, "How am I supposed to start making games if you won't give me a chance to do it?" Or, worse, imagine that your first job gives you three stars out of five, because you didn't have mentorship and training yet. Now imagine just how difficult it will be to get hired for your second project when you're competing with others who do have that coveted five-star rating. In a world of experts everywhere, all the time, there aren't huge incentives to provide opportunities and grace for people who are just learning.

Career Ladders
What about advancing in your chosen field? In many fields, as you gain more experience and skills, you gradually transition through different roles to learn new skills and open the door to new responsibilities. For example, beginning engineers are expected to be able to achieve a well-specified goal, but more advanced engineers are expected to be able to work with less well-defined goals in order to allow for more creativity and to develop unexpected solutions. That doesn't mesh with how online labor markets work, since you're typically hired for projects with specific goals. It can be costly to allow an engineer on an hourly rate to explore different solutions for a project. How do you develop your skills and climb the career ladder if you can only ever get hired for skills that you *already* have, rather than for growth opportunities? Traditionally, companies would invest in people for the medium to long term with the hope that they could grow the talent internally. But with that incentive erased, how do we enable those growth opportunities? Is it something the platform needs to take on?

Employee Morale
Look at the many issues with the gig economy as a preview of what might happen to a flash teams economy if we don't figure out a pro-social future for workers: one that enables people to get their first jobs, gain skills, and get paid fairly. Gig workers today tend to feel disaffected and disempowered.[5] Food delivery workers and cab drivers regularly go out on strike, and it's a career that they view as a temporary stopgap until their next stable job arrives or they find another job that pays more.

Or look back even farther, since many of these issues are like a bad rerun of the piecework economy from the mid-1800s. PhD student Ali Alkhatib, along with our faculty colleague Margaret Levi, examined these parallels in detail.[6] Historically, piecework payment—per piece of work completed—arose in a context of farms and textiles. For example, a worker might receive payment per garment sewn. Likewise, today we pay food delivery drivers per meal and pay Uber drivers per ride. Like today's workers, piecework workers found it to be a distasteful environment: they were pushed to their limit just to make a living wage, and their work was optimized until it removed most sense of holistic ownership or autonomy. Large and highly publicized strikes among piecework employees and others exploited in poor working conditions followed—for example, the matchgirls' strike in London in 1888, garment workers in Philadelphia in 1909, and coal miners in Pennsylvania in 1902. Worker rebellions led to the creation of labor advocacy groups and unions, and sometimes succeeded in winning better working conditions.

Using Platforms to Bring Together Firms and Workers

There is a huge opportunity for platforms to take these issues seriously. One example of a platform focused specifically on creating fair working conditions was the global collaboration of researchers known as the Stanford Crowd Research Collective. The collective created an online labor platform called Daemo that took on many of these issues and ideas. The collective created the boomerang-style reputational system and the crowd guilds approach that we will discuss in a moment.[7]

Daemo also took several interesting positions on policies. For one, it was constitutionally governed: workers, clients, and the platform developers all had seats at the table. There are lots of difficult questions to answer about how a constitutionally governed platform ought to work. For example, how active do people have to be in order to get a vote? What happens when workers and clients are at loggerheads? What if the workers and clients both want something that is practically impossible for the platform developers to build? Would the policies developed by these groups lead to a sustainable platform? It would be a big democratic experiment. The Daemo platform also instituted a policy on what it called *prototype tasks*.[8] Prototype tasks are a required soft launch for large-scale tasks: all tasks go to a set of workers for testing and feedback before they are launched to the entire marketplace.

If platforms like Daemo can work, they can demonstrate that many of the challenges we face in the future of work are failures of imagination, not engineering. In fact, a popular machine learning dataset called SQuAD 2.0 used Daemo for data collection.[9] Daemo is now shut down as a research project, but the ideas are ripe for folks to pick up.

Payment Protections and Fair Wages

On platforms such as Upwork, there are payment protections to prevent wage theft—a client cannot simply refuse to pay. Upwork also features an arbitration and appeals process for payment. On Amazon Mechanical Turk, however, no such protections exist. An online organizing group called "We Are Dynamo" took on this and other issues and produced a document recommending a specific minimum wage.[10] Pricing work correctly really is a skill, however, and many clients new to the arena don't have it yet. In surveys of Mechanical Turk workers, underpayment was the single most frequently cited complaint. Let's say that you estimate that someone can complete a task in about thirty minutes, but it actually tends to take people an hour. Then your effective wage will be half of what you intended because of this error in estimating how long the task will take.

Mark Whiting of Stanford took this issue and drove it to its logical conclusion: you should be specifying your target wage (i.e., intended hourly wage), not your piecework rate (i.e., how much you pay per task based on estimated time). He and team built a tool called Fair Work in which a worker self-reports how long a task takes.[11] Over time, if the program notices that the task is underpaid, it automatically sends bonuses to the workers to make sure that they make their target wage. Could workers intentionally over-report their time to make more money? Maybe, but in our estimation, it's less likely than an employer accidentally underpaying. If there are strategic manipulators, it's possible to identify much of the behavior with modern AI and data science tools.

Benefits

In countries such as the United States that connect benefits to employment, the traditional safety nets generally don't exist if you work online. Health care insurance, retirement savings, sick leave, disability leave, and other "guarantees" aren't actually guaranteed when you are an independent contractor. The National Domestic Workers Alliance, or NDWA, an advocacy organization for home care workers, house cleaners, and nannies, has begun pursuing interesting responses to this issue. NDWA's Fair Care Labs began a collaboration with Stanford PhD student Ali Alkhatib to investigate the possibility of portable benefits. Their resulting system, Alia, is a payment platform for domestic workers that automatically pulls in some portion of the payment to contribute to the worker's benefits.[12] This way, workers get contributions to their benefits from every client, essentially prorated by how much of their time that client has hired them, and they can draw from the pool of accrued benefits coverage when they need it. Domestic workers do not work remotely, but this is an interesting model for providing benefits for online workers.

Internships

What about career growth? There are opportunities for software to help here, too. One opportunity is what we might call micro-internships: the ability to take on short, paid, mentored, real-world work experiences in order to build skills and a resume.[13] Our team, led by visiting student (and now professor) Ryo Suzuki, created a system to facilitate micro-internships on Upwork. Typically, you as a worker might not get selected for a job, since you don't have the experience and ratings to be competitive. But when a company agrees to provide a micro-internship, our system identifies a potential mentor to oversee your work—someone who has a strong reputation in the area. They meet with you regularly, structure your work to include checkpoints, and give you feedback at each checkpoint. And they ultimately stand behind the quality of the work.

Micro-internships succeed because they are win-win. Workers, most obviously, get experience and payment. For their part, clients save money by taking on interns: it turns out to often be cheaper to hire an intern even if they will take more hours to complete the job, and even if we are paying for a few hours from an expensive expert to mentor them and provide oversight. In our experiments, we recruited mentors and interns to complete a nontrivial web engineering project of building an interactive web application for a company's e-commerce store over the course of a week. We observed that mentors made roughly their usual hourly advertised rates for the time they put in to mentor the intern, interns got access to work they would have not otherwise been eligible for, and interns learned many skills from their mentors along the way. About 25 percent of tasks on Upwork fulfill necessary criteria for a micro-internship: entry-level work with specific goals, concrete deliverables, and a non-urgent deadline.

Crowd Guilds and Accreditation

If we can build tools for internships, perhaps we can also build tools for accreditation. Crowd guilds allow workers to group together and stand behind each other's expertise.[14] As an example, a group of workers online might create a financial forecasting guild. If you're a financial forecaster, you join the guild in order to gain access to more work. You might start out at the ground level, a Level 1 member of the guild. Then, as you work, the crowd guilds system sends a random subset of your work to other members of the guild for double-blind peer review. In other words, higher-level members of the guild occasionally look at your work, without knowing that it's your work, to consider you for promotion. If your work warrants it, you become a Level 2 member, then Level 3, and so on. The higher your level, the higher a price your work can command.

The Crowd Research Collective ran a field experiment where we compared crowd guilds' reputational signals to the traditional ones you'd find on a platform, such as the percentage of successfully accepted work. We focused on creating a guild for common data annotation micro-tasks, and over the two weeks, nearly 200 workers completed over 15,000 such tasks as members of a crowd guild. The guild members' assessments of each other were more predictive of work quality than the traditional signals available on the platform—suggesting that not only can this approach benefit workers, it also yields better work.

We Are Dynamo: A Case Study in Organizing Online Workers

Some people diagnose a broader issue in the gig economy, which is the weakening of workers' collective power to ensure fair working conditions. Remote work and some kinds of contract work can complicate workers' ability to organize and negotiate with collective power. New York Times labor reporter Noam Scheiber made this point when he wrote about our flash teams research. In a social media discussion about his article on flash teams, Scheiber pointed out that Hollywood is all temporary organizations, but the workers do well.[15] Why, he asked? His answer: because workers are organized.

A group of researchers and organizers pursued a similar goal by creating We Are Dynamo, the first platform ever designed specifically for labor organizing of online workers.[16] We Are Dynamo contained a number of affordances that would be familiar to you as a member of any online platform today: it contained a feed where workers could suggest ideas (e.g., "Let's create a badge that clients who adhere to our guidelines can display"), an upvote and downvote mechanism for ideas, and a Kickstarter-style threshold for the minimum number of upvotes required to transform an idea into an outright campaign. The platform also contained some ideas that were unique to labor organizations: for example, it required verification that the member was an active worker on the Amazon Mechanical Turk platform.

Mechanical Turk organized a public letter-writing campaign to Amazon CEO Jeff Bezos aiming to humanize themselves to the public and draw attention to their goals and needs. The introduction to the campaign read, "This is a writing campaign for Turkers to let Jeff Bezos, head of Amazon and brainchild behind mTurk, and the rest of the world know all about who we are. The intent is to get Bezos to see that Turkers are not only actual human beings, but people who deserve respect, fair treatment and open communication." Their letter-writing campaign got the attention of international media sources including The Guardian, The Daily Beast, and two European radio stations.

We Are Dynamo also pressured academic researchers to establish better working conditions. Why? Amazon Mechanical Turk, it turns out, was a bit of a revolution for academic research in AI and the social sciences. Researchers used to struggle to find participants for lab experiments and to help them label training data for AI, often relying on students they knew. But, it turns out, Amazon Mechanical Turk was far more accessible and far more inclusive than many bodies of students, making the data easier to gather and more representative.

However, a lot of graduate-level students executing these studies had not been trained on how to be a good manager. Academics received a terrible reputation among the workers on Amazon Mechanical Turk because they paid poorly, gave poor instructions, and tended to reject work without explanation. So, the workers on We Are Dynamo collectively authored a 23-page set of guidelines for ethical research on Mechanical Turk. Their guidelines included recommended pay rates, how to handle work that you are dissatisfied with, and how to respect worker privacy. A number of university Institutional Review Boards (IRBs), the committees that review research ethics for all peer-reviewed research, began using these guidelines when reviewing research involving human subjects.

The complete story of We Are Dynamo needs to also acknowledge just how difficult it is to organize workers with an online platform. The internet makes it easy for people to gather online, yes, but it also makes it easy for those collectives to disperse. Many of the efforts on We Are Dynamo tilted between very heated fights on one hand, and lack of progress on the other. Workers had very different opinions on what ought to be done, and how, and there was no set of rules agreed on in advance for how to produce consensus. Still, We Are Dynamo provided templates for how future groups could address these issues productively.

What Can (and Can't) Policy Fix?

The future is here, but it's not looking very evenly distributed. Upwork's most recent statistics estimate that 38 percent of Americans engaged in freelance work in the past year, amounting to one and a quarter trillion dollars of contributions to the economy.[17] With over one third of Americans engaging in freelancing, and the likely outcome that more and more of this will move online over time, it is urgent that we develop policy intervention to shape these outcomes pro-socially. It's in everyone's best interests to ensure that the best workers feel comfortable engaging in freelancing and flash teams work. It's not clear that, at least here in America, the state and federal policy levers have moved yet to shape this future effectively.

One of our takeaways from a decade of research on the future of work is that you can build all the prosocial technology you want, but there's nothing requiring companies to use it. Micro-internships, fair wage tools, and collective action platforms aren't of much use if they aren't broadly accessible. And traditional approaches in computing don't work.

A nonprofit once built a paid crowdsourced video annotation platform that was open source, meaning that the code was public and anybody could run it. This annotation platform included features and controls to help ensure that workers were paid fairly for their work. Open source software is generally seen as a stamp of being "good for the world," since the software is released freely for anyone to use and build on. But a for-profit startup took this open source code, stripped it of all its features and controls for fair pay, and created a closed company that undercut the nonprofit on prices—markets doing what markets do. The nonprofit couldn't sustain itself and eventually collapsed. When we talked to the tech founder of the nonprofit, he was disillusioned. He did the right things, creating prosocial innovations in his platform and open sourcing the platform, only to find his prosocial "bits" flipped off at the whim of someone else.

This is where government policy can step in. Code cannot solve issues on its own. It can create opportunities, but it cannot compel usage or shared behavior.[18] That's exactly what law does: it creates and enforces shared expectations. And we can design policy just like we design code. Then the question becomes: what should be regulated, and what should not?

So far, in the United States and Europe, the move has largely been in terms of worker classification. Traditionally, there have been two major classes of workers: employees and self-employed independent contractors. Employees are typically entitled to all sorts of benefits and rights, whereas independent contractors are not formally employed by the organization but have increased control over the work they do and how much they do. This is a difference that matters: employees, but not contractors, gain access to benefits such as retirement, health care insurance (in the United States), and paid leave. As we write this, the US Department of Labor has proposed rules that classify workers in the gig economy as employees rather than contractors, changing the nature of benefits they are entitled to. Likewise, the European Union passed a Platform Worker Directive that helps shape worker classification decisions. There is legitimate policy debate to be had about whether what we need here is to (1) classify workers as employees, (2) reshape the existing self-employed classification policies to better match the needs and reality of modern gig workers, or (3) craft a third classification that blends the two classic models.

To come back to where we started, innovation is held back when technology and policy can't create prosocial outcomes. Each upcoming generation of entrepreneurs gets excited about changing the world. It turns out that, when they can't produce a vision of a positive future, they go elsewhere. If there were certainty that they could be creating a new generation of good jobs, many would be attracted. But right now, there remains a lot of uncertainty on our campus around whether building gig economy software leads to a better world. When we talk to Stanford students, there's just too much trepidation about what they'd be creating.

Let's return to our North Star of creating opportunities that workers would prefer to equivalent traditional work. Could we require that platforms direct additional payments into a portable benefits pool, to help ensure that the workers we hire maintain basic needs? Could we create new worker classification types that recognize the fluid nature of this new form of work, and properly reward it? Could we place clearer requirements on the conditions for work rejection to avoid wage theft? What else can we do to reduce the risk that highly talented workers see when they consider joining this future of work?

If we do nothing, incredible opportunities will be offset by a replay of the piecework of the past. States and nations that create innovative policies will be miles ahead in crafting the future of work. If we want to create systems that help us convene the right collaborators; if we want to create systems that help us find the right way to collaborate; if we want to create systems that empower anyone—entrepreneurs, civil society, volunteer organizations—with the ability to convene a group around themselves in minutes, then we need to create policy that recognizes that this is exciting not because it is access to cheap labor, but because it enables dramatic new forms of collaboration between diverse participants online.

18 Conclusion: A Bridge from Here to There

Eliza joined a conference dedicated to the future of collaboration technology. Seemed like a timely experiment! The conference was to take place entirely online in a virtual space set up to mirror the physical layout of an in-person conference. There were rooms in the conference space, attendees were represented by virtual avatars, and you could walk your avatar over to a room to hear a presentation.

Because the conference was distributed globally across many time zones, talk times would inevitably have been at 3:00 am for someone, so none of the talks were live: they were prerecorded videos repeated a few times. To attend a talk, you could walk into a room with the prerecorded talk and stand near the screen, which would play a YouTube video of the talk recording. If you wanted to talk live to someone else at the conference, you navigated your avatar over next to their avatar.

And yet—the place was an absolute ghost town. If you saw someone who you were interested in talking to, chances were that their avatar was just idly standing in one place because they had closed their laptop and started doing something else. Eliza's talk was attended by perhaps one live participant.

Was this the future of distributed collaboration for flash teams?

We've all heard too many proclamations about remote work, hybrid work, and the future of work. It's undeniable that we are now living careers that corporations would have rejected out of hand as recently as a few years ago. Nearly a third of paid workdays have a work-from-home arrangement.[1] Working from home is valued as much as a 15 percent salary increase.[2] While many corporations and managers have embraced a hybrid or fully remote workforce, they have not yet done the work to make the most out of this new model.

We argue that the remote work transformation of organizations is incomplete. Today's conversations focus too narrowly around working from home. What these conversations are missing is that remote work has opened the door to a broad new class of organizations that take full advantage of the fact that some or all members are remote 100 percent of the time.

Imagine not just a flash team but an entire flash organization. It can react in minutes to any need by bringing on new experts or reconfiguring its org chart; it can draw on spare moments of world experts' insights; it can experiment on itself and learn continuously. How might these organizations compete for talent? How might workers' experiences shift? What kinds of new policies will we need?

Today, your colleagues aren't thinking about the flash organization or the evolution of the organization, because they are still duct-taping the design of today's organizations onto the new reality of hybrid work. We have continued to design hybrid and remote work patterned after traditional teams or organizations. Organizational charts haven't changed; our tools are still rough analogues of in-person collaboration strategies; and how we hire, train, and collaborate still looks similar to how it did a decade ago. It's like we invented the most powerful race car engine in the world and then were so short-sighted that we designed the chassis around it to look like a Honda Odyssey.

This chapter takes up the question: why are we being so short-sighted? And what might it look like if we weren't?

Being There

Organizations are a technology for organizing people, and that technology at a fundamental level hasn't really changed much since the Industrial Revolution. They arose in their modern form as a way to coordinate railroads across large distances: railroads were the first time humanity had needed to organize its efforts over such large geographic and labor scales.[3] To achieve this, the first organizational designers looked for inspiration from the most modern technologies they had at hand. And as it turns out, the most advanced technology of the time was mechanical devices. Just like a clock tower is a complex interlinking of many gears, organizations were designed to similarly link workers' interdependent efforts. We inherit this thinking even in modern management treatments like Dalio's *Principles*, which explicitly thinks of organizations as machines.[4] It's no wonder that we are seen as "cogs in a machine": that was literally the original goal.

Imagine the changes that have happened in human technology during the 200 years since the original organizational designers looked to mechanical gears as the most advanced technology for their inspiration. In those two centuries, computing went from a gleam in the eye of its originator Charles Babbage into something so powerful and compact that we can wear it as a watch on our wrists. Computing's metaphors—desktops, search, natural language—and its affordances look nothing like either Babbage's visions in the 1820s nor like the mechanical devices and steam engines of the time. So why do our organizations still work the same?

Organizations *are* technologies, yes, and just like any technology, they can be redesigned and reinvented. As technologies, some organizations amplify us more than others. Yochai Benkler at Harvard Law School and others have documented thoroughly how online collaboration led to dramatically new forms of organization that produced Wikipedia and the Linux operating system.[5] So what organizations might lie around the corner?

If you look around you, the news and technology industries will have you believe that the future we are creating is one that's about "being there": aiming to recreate the experience of sitting next to your collaborator in real life. Slack's marketing material proclaims "Collaborate with your team online as easily as you do in person."[6] Not to be outdone, Google's announcement for its Project Starline tech demo screams, "Feel like you're there, together."[7] UC San Francisco's IT department is a bit more pragmatic, advising, "How to have a Zoom meeting that is (almost) as good as being there."[8] The news media buy into this, too: in reporting on the videoconferencing solutions of DreamWorks animation, FastCompany titled their article simply, "Being There."[9]

Too many organizations today aim for "being there." In our view, this aim is misguided at best and harmful at worst. Jim Hollan and Scott Stornetta, two researchers at communications technology lab Bellcore, realized this fact decades before most of us.[10] Bellcore was building video telecommunications technology back in 1992. Looking at empirical results from what was, at that point, likely the most advanced video collaboration system in the world, Hollan and Stornetta had a close-up view as this future was coming into focus. And they weren't impressed. The field was moving toward better resolution, less latency, and generally more impressive technology. Yet people weren't feeling closer together. What was going on?

The problem is that there are fundamental limits to whether technology can ever be as good as being there. For starters, the internet typically takes about 75 milliseconds to send signals between the West and East Coasts of the United States. This delay is inevitable: even if data were to travel at the speed of light, it would take 40 milliseconds to travel that distance.[11] That means that when you finish speaking in California, there will always be a delay before you see your partner in Massachusetts respond: first, the data needs to get over to them, then they need to respond, and their response needs to make its way back to you.

That blip of a delay screws up our natural turn-taking when speaking. Our brains interpret these extra time gaps in all sorts of confusing ways, either implying that we should keep talking, or as awkward silence. And if we ever do colonize the moon, that distance-induced lag will become a minimum of 1.3 seconds—imagine the unbearable tension for over two and a half seconds after you tell your significant other on the moon "I love you" and before you see their reaction. No amount of VR immersion is ever going to overcome that.

Reimagining Work

So, stop trying to replicate "being there," and stop trying to make modern organizations look like an online version of in-person work. Have you ever seen a favorite book, show, or video game turned into a terrible movie? One of the cardinal sins is asking a movie to succeed by leaning into the same elements that makes the book tick. Different media require different artistic decisions. Peter Jackson's *Lord of the Rings* movies had to drop a huge amount of background worldbuilding in the books, and instead aimed for a sense of scale through scenery and visuals. This was Hollan and Stornetta's original point: don't try to run the same race as in-person collaboration—instead, run a race that in-person collaboration could never win.[12] Don't try to make remote collaboration less worse; instead, find dimensions in which remote collaboration will always be better, and lean into those.

Flash teams focus on what kinds of work can only happen through hybrid and remote work. What does remote work do better than in-person

Conclusion

work? What kinds of teams and organizational forms take advantage of what is better and unique about remote work? What superpowers does remote work grant an organization?

This is going "beyond being there." Going beyond being there means running a different race. In-person organizations will continue to be good at the things that they excel at: building of familiarity and trust, rapid-fire brainstorming and decision-making, and ad-hoc watercooler conversations. Trying to meet or beat traditional organizations at these games is typically a losing proposition: you might remember Zoom happy hours, Gather.town hangouts, and shared whiteboards in video calls that all felt awkward at best and ham-fisted at worst.

So instead, ask yourself: what are the dimensions that remote work excels at, and traditional organizations will never be able to match? We view flash teams as one answer to that question, but let's examine the principle of the thing.

Ability of flash teams	Going "beyond being there" with that ability
Experts everywhere Instant reach to a global workforce	Getting exactly the expertise that you need, exactly at the time that you need it
Elastic organizations Rapidly changeable organization size and boundaries	Small organizations operating with the skill and scale of large organizations when desired
Expert office hours Micro-moments of expertise	Call on fifteen minutes of help or advising from experts at any time
Trusted experts Ratings and feedback	Less risk in bringing on external experts

Let's look at each of these affordances in more detail.

Experts everywhere. This affordance is key to flash teams—it is the connection to a globally networked workforce, where nearly anything you're looking for is available quickly. *Experts everywhere* is a mindset that takes some time to adapt to: it requires shifting from an expertise-scarcity mindset to an expertise-abundance mindset.

Experts everywhere provide many opportunities that are not just about flash teams as we've described them. Ultimately, the core affordance is that you can recruit exactly the kind of expertise you're looking for, right when you need it. We have stretched this concept to its logical conclusion with flash teams, imagining remote-only teams that recruit on demand. But there are many other ways you might take advantage of experts everywhere. For example, it might help your organization hire someone temporarily when you have a need, while you run a broader search for a permanent addition. Or, it might allow you to bring in a part-time expert to help advise you on making a permanent hire. It might even allow you to bring in that expert to help do an external review of your own team's work. Or they might help with focused needs: maybe an employee disagreement spiraled into a big dispute, and you can bring in an expert mediator to help.

Elastic organizations. In computing, "elastic" resources are resources that you can ask for on demand when needed. For example, if your platform is getting a lot of traffic, you can spin up elastic server resources from Amazon Web Services or Google Cloud to help handle the load, without needing to buy a permanent new server.

Now imagine that your organization can become similarly elastic. Flash teams are focused on rapid reconfiguration and growth, but again there are many ways your organization can become more nimble and reconfigurable. Often, small organizations hire generalists because they need people to play multiple roles—but elastic organizations might also let you bring in hyper-specialized experts to help get one part of the job done. While paying careful attention to software engineer Fred Brooks' famous exhortation that adding more people to a software project often makes it even later, your teams can get the superpower to expand and contract as needed.[13]

On-demand experts. Are you stuck? What if an expert were just a click away? When you're in a typical organization, the expert is probably already busy. But at a global scale, there's likely somebody who has a moment. No matter how skilled we are, we all benefit from advice from a peer or mentor. In writing this book, we consulted with senior colleagues. What if we could bring in an on-demand editor to help review a few paragraphs, or a chapter, right as we finish writing it? This doesn't displace the value of our book's staff editor, and would certainly lead to a better overall book. What if engineers could ask for quick advice when something isn't working? What if musicians could ask for quick feedback on a part of their performance?

On-demand experts are quick, targeted, and to the point. If you're stuck or want feedback, you swing by. But instead of being limited to just a rare meeting, these on-demand experts can, in principle, be called upon whenever you need them. Now, there is a risk that it would take longer to explain your problem to a new expert than it would take you to solve it, but good mentors know exactly which questions to ask to get to the heart of the issue quickly. Expert office hours are an example of how distance collaboration might put us in tighter, not looser, collaboration loops than in-person work.

Trusted experts. Companies invest a lot of energy in hiring. As well they should: whether to invest in a person is one of the most important decisions that an organization faces. The world of flash teams doesn't fundamentally change this calculus, but it does offer a tantalizing opportunity to reduce risk. When we began working with online platforms, we made some hires who didn't have the expertise that they advertised. At this point, though, platforms such as Upwork have developed far better signals—and we have not landed a dud when using them.

If your organization could have stronger trust in someone's expertise, how might it change your decision making? In some cases, perhaps not at all: hiring a full-time employee still ought to remain a careful decision. In many cases, however, the signal from an online platform might let you take more risks with a temporary hire. If you really are facing a crunch in your financial transaction processing department, being able to hire a set of people without worrying about how it will go can be a real benefit. The vetting provided by online platforms can give you the confidence that the expert you hire has provided excellent work to previous clients before you.

You'll Need More and Better-Quality Data

In addition to organizations taking this remote work future seriously, we think the second real problem to bridge to get to the vision of AI-augmented teams has to do with data.

Consider: why haven't traditional organizations already made use of these envisioned AI-driven, data-fed improvement cycles? Artificial intelligence needs data, and without high-quality data about lots of teams, AI cannot easily help us. AI can't aid teams when so much of our teaming happens outside of the view of algorithms. Yes, your organization probably has information about its teams, like its organization chart or the teams' quarterly objectives and key results. But we all know how little those on-paper documents reflect the day-to-day reality of our organizations. The last thing you'd want is an algorithm making recommendations based on some idealized vision of how teams work on paper instead of how they actually work.

This lack of data is fundamentally a social issue, not a technical one. It's because, unlike most goals where data science and AI have already succeeded, good data about teams is not plentiful. Instead, we fall prey to what's called Grudin's Paradox: the people who know the most about the team's situation are the least incentivized to record that information for an algorithm. Typically, it's the managers who care that team information is kept up to date.[14] On the other hand, the team members—the ones who actually have the on-the-ground knowledge of the team's status—always have more urgent things to do. Grudin's Paradox rears its ugly head in many aspects of organizational life: Who keeps the organization's wikis and documentation up to date? Who tracks the team's goals during a quarter? In this case, it's in nobody's individual best interest to spend time curating a play-by-play database of team information.

In a new world, we need new roles. Your organization will need to build out HR data science to make sure that your teams capture and leverage their collaboration data. These data scientists will be organizational archivists of a kind, helping you learn from the successes and mistakes of the past.

What Can You Launch Now?

Being a researcher in computing is thrilling because we get to live in the future. The Computing Research Association occasionally analyzes the patterns of diffusion of innovations from research labs into billion-dollar industries. Across domains such as mobile networking, microprocessors, personal computing, cloud computing, and robotics, there is typically a 20–50 year gap between when academic labs begin working on a topic and when it is mature enough to be a billion-dollar industry.[15] The Dartmouth workshop that is widely viewed as the founding of AI as a field, for example, was in 1956, and it wasn't until late 2022 that ChatGPT brought AI suddenly to the forefront of nearly every industry's attention. (AI, of course, had been integrated into many products long before that—Google search, cell phone cameras, cars—but ChatGPT feels like it was AI's coming-out party.)

Many of the examples in part two of this book were research systems. They're not products you can buy today. But that also doesn't mean that you have to wait 50 years for them. As we demonstrated here, they are already achievable with today's technology. But they don't have off-the-shelf solutions available yet.

This leaves you with a few practical paths for integrating AI into your teams. One is to wait until some of these technologies become productized by a startup or software company, then buy their software-as-a-service system. That's basically playing the waiting game, and as Homer Simpson puts it, "The waiting game sucks."[16] So a second option, if you have data scientists or AI experts on staff, or can hire a flash team, is to build these systems yourself in house and deploy them—just as Gigster did with karma. The academic research is sufficiently advanced at this point that you can use it as a blueprint for your own solutions. Ultimately, internal tooling is going to be the likely route for most large organizations, especially if they're training on private internal worker data. Given what we've seen over our last decade of work on flash teams, we are confident that you now have the tools to do so effectively.

And hey, if you are independently wealthy and want to accelerate some of these directions by funding our research, we won't argue. You know how to reach us.

Acknowledgments

This book would not have been possible without the invaluable support, insights, and encouragement from a community of incredible students. First, we acknowledge and thank the talented and insightful Daniela Retelny Blum for seeing the Flash Teams vision in our respective work and connecting us to get the whole thing started. We extend deepest gratitude to PhD students whose dedication and hard work have been instrumental in this journey: Beleicia Bullock, Carolyn Zou, Catherine Mullings, Dora Zhao, Joon Sung Park, Jordan Troutman, Lindsay Popowski, Michelle Lam, Omar Shaikh, Amanda Pratt, Adrienne Baer. We are profoundly grateful to our postdoctoral researchers, whose innovative thinking and relentless pursuit of excellence have significantly enriched this work: Farnaz Jahanbakhsh, Quinn Waess, Tiziano Piccardi, and Zivvy Epstein. A special thanks to our PhD alumni, who have gone on to achieve remarkable success and continue to inspire us with their accomplishments: Mitchell Gordon, Ranjay Krishna, Geza Kovacs, Niloufar Salehi, Ethan Fast, Justin Cheng, Joy Kim, Chinmay Kulkarni, Katharina Lix, Hatim Rahman, Rebecca Hinds, Abisola Kusimo. We also wish to acknowledge the exceptional contributions of our postdoctoral alumni, who have become leaders in their fields: Chenyan Jia, Joseph Seering, Amy X. Zhang, Mark Whiting, Jen Rhymer, and Nicolas Kokkalis. Thank you as well to Eric Lupfer, Catherine Woods, Lisa Pinto, and The Book Highlights Team for improving this book and bringing it to life. This research was supported by the National Science Foundation, Sloan Foundation, Accenture ATL, Microsoft, Toyota Research Institute, Stanford Cyber Initiative, Office of Naval Research, DARPA, Hasso Plattner Design Thinking Program, and Precourt Institute.

To Erin: for being my love, my family, and a true partner in all things. To Elena, Ellie, Eliza, Isaac: for making it all worth it and for making life so much fun.

To Adi: I couldn't have done this without you. Thank you for your support and patience. To Kai and Tavi, thank you for keeping me grounded and bringing joy to every day. You remind me of what truly matters.

Notes

Chapter 1

1. We will refer to ourselves using our last names in this book, because Valentine has a truly excellent last name.—Bernstein

2. Ronald H Coase, "The Nature of the Firm," *economica* 4, no. 16 (1937).

3. G.F. Davis, *The Vanishing American Corporation: Navigating the Hazards of a New Economy* (Berrett-Koehler Publishers, 2016).

4. Davis, *The Vanishing American Corporation*, xv.

Chapter 2

1. Steven J. Davis, R. Jason Faberman, and John C. Haltiwanger, "The Establishment-Level Behavior of Vacancies and Hiring," *The Quarterly Journal of Economics* 128, no. 2 (2013).

2. Nicolas Kokkalis et al., "EmailValet: Managing Email Overload Through Private, Accountable Crowdsourcing," *Proceedings of the 2013 Conference on Computer Supported Cooperative Work*, San Antonio, February 2013. Association for Computing Machinery.

3. https://tinyurl.com/emailvalet

4. M.L. Gray and S. Suri, *Ghost Work: How to Stop Silicon Valley from Building a New Global Underclass* (Harper Business, 2019).

5. Eric Colson, "Curiosity-Driven Data Science," *Harvard Business Review*, November 27, 2018, https://hbr.org/2018/11/curiosity-driven-data-science.

6. Melissa A. Valentine, Steven M. Asch, and Esther Ahn, "Who Pays the Cancer Tax? Patients Narratives in a Movement to Change their Invisible Work," *Organization Science* 34, no. 4 (2023).

7. Valentine et al., "Who Pays the Cancer Tax?"

8. Shannon Winter, "A Product Marketer Walks into a Marketing Analytics Team," LinkedIn, November 21, 2019, https://www.linkedin.com/pulse/product-marketer-walks-marketing-analytics-team-shannon-winter/.

Chapter 3

1. B. A. Bechky, "Gaffers, Gofers, and Grips: Role-Based Coordination in Temporary Organizations," *Organization Science* 17, no. 1 (Jan-Feb 2006), https://doi.org/10.1287/orsc.1050.0149.

2. M. A. Valentine and A. C. Edmondson, "Team Scaffolds: How Mesolevel Structures Enable Role-Based Coordination in Temporary Groups," *Organization Science* 26, no. 2 (2015), https://doi.org/10.1287/orsc.2014.0947.

3. Katharina Lucia Maria Lix, "Mixed-Method Approaches to Employment Relationships in Team-Based Online Gig Work" (PhD Diss., Stanford University, 2021), 68–69, https://purl.stanford.edu/rm124wf4080.

4. Peter Pirolli, *Information Foraging Theory: Adaptive Interaction with Information*, Human Technology Interaction Series, (Oxford University Press, 2009).

5. Jen Rhymer, "Location-Independent Organizations: Designing Collaboration Across Space and Time," *Administrative Science Quarterly* 68, no. 1 (2023), https://doi.org/10.1177/00018392221129175.

Chapter 4

1. Jeffrey Dastin, "Insight—Amazon Scraps Secret AI Recruiting Tool That Showed Bias against Women," *Reuters*, October 10, 2018, https://www.reuters.com/article/us-amazon-com-jobs-automation-insight/amazon-scraps-secret-ai-recruiting-tool-that-showed-bias-against-women/.

2. Spencer Soper, "Fired by Bot at Amazon: 'It's You Against the Machine'," *Bloomberg*, June 28, 2021. https://www.bloomberg.com/news/features/2021-06-28/fired-by-bot-amazon-turns-to-machine-managers-and-workers-are-losing-out.

3. Melissa A. Valentine et al., "Flash Organizations: Crowdsourcing Complex Work by Structuring Crowds As Organizations," *Proceedings of the 2017 CHI Conference on Human Factors in Computing Systems*, Denver, 2017. Association for Computing Machinery.

Chapter 5

1. A "P.O. challenge" is a medical procedure that involves a patient eating or drinking to determine if they are well enough to go home.

Notes

2. S. Wuchty, B. F. Jones, and B. Uzzi, "The Increasing Dominance of Teams in Production of Knowledge," *Science* 316, no. 5827 (May 2007), https://doi.org/10.1126/science.1136099.

3. Amy Edmondson, *Teaming: How Organizations Learn, Innovate, and Compete in the Knowledge Economy* (Wiley, 2012).

4. Melissa A. Valentine and Amy C. Edmondson, "Team Scaffolds: How Mesolevel Structures Enable Role-Based Coordination in Temporary Groups," *Organization Science* 26, no. 2 (2015): 405–422.

5. Melissa Valentine, "When Equity Seems Unfair: The Role of Justice Enforceability in Temporary Team Coordination," *Academy of Management Journal* 61, no. 6 (2018).

6. Ruth Wageman, J. Richard Hackman, and Erin Lehman, "Team Diagnostic Survey: Development of an Instrument," *The Journal of Applied Behavioral Science* 41, no. 4 (2005).

Chapter 6

1. Josh Darnit, "Exact Instructions Challenge—THIS Is Why My Kids Hate Me. | Josh Darnit," YouTube video, 6:45, uploaded January 26, 2017, https://youtu.be/cDA3_5982h8.

2. Daniela Retelny, Michael S Bernstein, and Melissa A. Valentine, "No Workflow Can Ever Be Enough: How Crowdsourcing Workflows Constrain Complex Work," *Proceedings of the ACM on Human-Computer Interaction* 1, no. CSCW (2017).

3. Marissa Webb, "Selective Attention Test," YouTube video, 5:12, uploaded January 11, 2018, https://youtu.be/_bnnmWYI0lM.

4. Li Lu, Y. Connie Yuan, and Poppy Lauretta McLeod, "Twenty-Five Years of Hidden Profiles in Group Decision Making: A Meta-Analysis," *Personality and Social Psychology Review* 16, no. 1 (2012), https://doi.org/10.1177/1088868311417243.

5. Amy C. Edmondson, *Teaming: How Organizations Learn, Innovate, and Compete in the Knowledge Economy* (Wiley, 2012).

Chapter 7

1. Melissa A. Valentine et al., "Flash Organizations: Crowdsourcing Complex Work by Structuring Crowds As Organizations," *Proceedings of the 2017 CHI Conference on Human Factors in Computing Systems*, Denver, 2017. Association for Computing Machinery.

2. "GitHub: Let's build from here · GitHub." https://github.com/.

Chapter 8

1. This vignette is an anonymized version of what we saw happen to two teams, Alpha and Bravo, that both had to build a new app feature for a high-profile client.

2. *The Fugitive*, directed by Andrew Davis (Warner Bros., 1993) 2:10.

3. *The Fugitive*.

4. Noam Scheiber, "The Pop-Up Employer: Build a Team, Do the Job, Say Goodbye," *New York Times*, July 12, 2017.

5. Katharina Lucia Maria Lix, "Mixed-Method Approaches to Employment Relationships in Team-Based Online Gig Work" (PhD diss., Stanford University, 2021), 68–69, https://purl.stanford.edu/rm124wf4080.

6. Lix, "Mixed Method Approaches," 69.

7. Lix, 69.

8. Lix, 69.

9. Lix, 69.

10. Herbert A. Simon, "The Architecture of Complexity," *Proceedings of the American Philosophical Society* 106, no. 6 (1962): 467–482, https://www.jstor.org/stable/985254.

11. R. Gulati and H. Singh, "The Architecture of Cooperation: Managing Coordination Costs and Appropriation Concerns in Strategic Alliances," *Administrative Science Quarterly* 43, no. 4 (1998), https://doi.org/10.2307/2393616.

12. Lix, "Mixed-Method Approaches."

13. Lix, 77.

14. Lix, 81.

Chapter 9

1. Melissa A. Valentine, "Renegotiating Spheres of Obligation: The Role of Hierarchy in Organizational Learning," *Administrative Science Quarterly* 63, no. 3 (2017), https://doi.org/10.1177/0001839217718547.

2. Robert I. Sutton, *The No Asshole Rule: Building a Civilized Workplace and Surviving One That Isn't* (Grand Central Publishing, 2007).

3. Robert I. Sutton, *Good Boss, Bad Boss: How to Be the Best . . . and Learn from the Worst* (Grand Central Publishing, 2010).

4. Bob Sutton, "Hierarchy is Good. Hierarchy is Essential. And Less Isn't Always Better," Stanford Technology Ventures Program, April 7, 2016, https://ecorner

.stanford.edu/articles/hierarchy-is-good-hierarchy-is-essential-and-less-isnt-always-better/.

5. Sutton, "Hierarchy is Good."

6. Amy C. Edmondson, "Psychological Safety and Learning Behavior in Work Teams," *Administrative Science Quarterly* 44, no. 2 (1999): 350–383, http://www.jstor.org/stable/2666999.

Chapter 10

1. Jonathan P. Chang, Justin Cheng, and Cristian Danescu-Niculescu-Mizil, "Don't Let Me Be Misunderstood: Comparing Intentions and Perceptions in Online Discussions," *Proceedings of The Web Conference 2020*, Tapei, 2020. Association for Computing Machinery.

2. Hatim A. Rahman and Melissa A. Valentine, "How Managers Maintain Control Through Collaborative Repair: Evidence from Platform-Mediated 'Gigs'," *Organization Science* 32, no.5 (2021), https://doi.org/10.1287/orsc.2021.1428.

3. Emily D. Heaphy, "Repairing Breaches with Rules: Maintaining Institutions in the Face of Everyday Disruptions," *Organization Science* 24, no. 5 (2013), https://doi.org/10.1287/orsc.1120.0798.

4. Rahman and Valentine, "How Managers Maintain Control Through Collaborative Repair," 16.

5. Rahman and Valentine, 16.

6. Rahman and Valentine, 17.

7. Rahman and Valentine, 17.

8. Rahman and Valentine, 18.

9. Rahman and Valentine, 19.

10. Pamela J. Hinds and Diane E. Bailey, "Out of Sight, Out of Sync: Understanding Conflict in Distributed Teams," *Organization Science* 14, no. 6 (2003): 615–758, https://doi.org/10.1287/orsc.14.6.615.24872.

11. M. S. Silberman et al., "Responsible Research With Crowds: Pay Crowdworkers At Least Minimum Wage," *Communications of the ACM* 61, no. 3 (2018), https://doi.org/10.1145/3180492.

12. Brian McInnis et al., "Taking a HIT: Designing around Rejection, Mistrust, Risk, and Workers' Experiences in Amazon Mechanical Turk," *Proceedings of the 2016 CHI Conference on Human Factors in Computing Systems*, San Jose, California, 2016. Association for Computing Machinery.

Chapter 11

1. Min Kyung Lee et al., "Working with Machines: The Impact of Algorithmic and Data-Driven Management on Human Workers," *Proceedings of the 33rd Annual ACM Conference on Human Factors in Computing Systems*, Seoul, Republic of Korea, 2015. Association for Computing Machinery; Gray and Suri, *Ghost Work*.

2. David Martin et al., "Being a Turker," *Proceedings of the 17th ACM Conference on Computer Supported Cooperative Work and Social Computing*, Baltimore, Maryland, 2014. Association for Computing Machinery; Gray and Suri, *Ghost Work*; Lilly C. Irani and M. Silberman, "Turkopticon: Interrupting Worker Invisibility in Amazon Mechanical Turk," *Proceedings of the SIGCHI Conference on Human Factors in Computing Systems*, Paris, 2013. Association for Computing Machinery; McInnis et al., "Taking a HIT: Designing Around Rejection, Mistrust, Risk, and Workers' Experiences in Amazon Mechanical Turk," *Proceedings of the 2016 CHI Conference on Human Factors in Computing Systems*, San Jose, 2016. Association for Computing Machinery.

3. Apostolos Filippas, John Joseph Horton, and Joseph Golden, "Reputation Inflation" *Proceedings of the 2018 ACM Conference on Economics and Computation*, Ithaca, NY, 2018. Association for Computing Machinery.

4. S. S. Gaikwad et al., "Boomerang: Rebounding the Consequences of Reputation Feedback on Crowdsourcing Platforms," *Proceedings of the 29th Annual ACM Symposium on User Interface Software and Technology*, New York, 2016. Association for Computing Machinery.

5. Thomas Ma et al., "Balancing Producer Fairness and Efficiency via Prior-Weighted Rating System Design," (2023), arXiv preprint.

6. Hatim A. Rahman, "The Invisible Cage: Workers' Reactivity to Opaque Algorithmic Evaluations," *Administrative Science Quarterly* 66, no. 4 (2021), https://doi.org/10.1177/00018392211010118.

7. Rahman, "The Invisible Cage: Workers' Reactivity to Opaque Algorithmic Evaluations," 957.

8. Rahman, "The Invisible Cage," 957.

9. Katharina Lix and Melissa A. Valentine "When a Bot Scores Your Karma: Algorithmic Ranking Systems as Uncertainty Reducers in Platform Gig Work," (2020), Stanford University, Working Paper. https://mvalentine.github.io/pdfs/karma.pdf.

10. Lix and Valentine, "When a Bot Scores Your Karma," 21.

11. Lix and Valentine, 23.

12. Lix and Valentine, 25.

13. Lix and Valentine, 116, 117.

14. Lix and Valentine, 27.

15. Christina A. Pan et al., "Comparing the Perceived Legitimacy of Content Moderation Processes: Contractors, Algorithms, Expert Panels, and Digital Juries," *Proceedings of the ACM on Human-Computer Interaction* 6, no. 82 (2022). https://doi.org/10.1145/3512929.

Chapter 12

1. R. Bohn, "From Art to Science in Manufacturing: The Evolution of Technological Knowledge," *Foundations and Trends in Technology, Information, and Operations Management* 1, no. 2 (2005).

2. M. McInnis et al., "Taking a HIT: Designing Around Rejection, Mistrust, Risk, and Workers' Experiences in Amazon Mechanical Turk," *Proceedings of the 2016 CHI Conference on Human Factors in Computing Systems*, San Jose, 2016. Association for Computing Machinery.

3. Lix and Valentine, "When a Bot Scores your Karma: Algorithmic Ranking Systems as Uncertainty Reducers in Platform Gig Work," 115.

4. Anita Williams Woolley et al., "Evidence for a Collective Intelligence Factor in the Performance of Human Groups," *Science* 330, no. 6004 (2010), https://doi.org/10.1126/science.1193147.

5. Diane Wei Liang, Richard Moreland, and Linda Argote, "Group Versus Individual Training and Group Performance: The Mediating Factor of Transactive Memory," *Personality and Social Psychology Bulletin* 21, no. 4 (1995), https://doi.org/10.1177/0146167295214009; R. Reagans, L. Argote, and D. Brooks, "Individual Experience and Experience Working Together: Predicting Learning Rates From Knowing Who Knows What and Knowing How to Work Together," *Management Science* 51, no. 6 (2005), https://doi.org/10.1287/mnsc.1050.0366.

6. Lu Hong and Scott E. Page, "Groups of Diverse Problem Solvers Can Outperform Groups of High-Ability Problem Solvers," *Proceedings of the National Academy of Sciences* 101, no. 46 (2004), https://doi.org/doi:10.1073/pnas.0403723101; Scott E. Page, *The Difference: How the Power of Diversity Creates Better Groups, Firms, Schools, and Societies* (Princeton University Press, 2008).

7. Hong and Page, "Groups of Diverse Problem Solvers Can Outperform Groups of High-Ability Problem Solvers."

8. Niloufar Salehi et al., "Huddler: Convening Stable and Familiar Crowd Teams Despite Unpredictable Availability," *Proceedings of the 2017 ACM Conference on Computer-Supported Cooperative Work and Social Computing* (ACM, 2017).

9. Niloufar Salehi and Michael S. Bernstein, "Hive: Collective Design Through Network Rotation," *Proceedings of the ACM on Human-Computer Interaction* 2, no. CSCW (2018), https://doi.org/10.1145/3274420.

10. Salehi et al., "Huddler."

11. Salehi et al., 1709.

12. Salehi et al., 1710.

13. Diego Gómez-Zará et al., "Who Would You Like to Work With?," *Proceedings of the 2019 CHI Conference on Human Factors in Computing Systems*, Glasgow, Scotland, 2019. Association for Computing Machinery; Alexa M. Harris et al., "Joining Together Online: The Trajectory of CSCW Scholarship on Group Formation," *Proceedings of the ACM on Human-Computer Interaction* 3, no. CSCW (2019), https://doi.org/10.1145/3359250; Diego Gómez-Zará, Leslie A. DeChurch, and Noshir S. Contractor, "A Taxonomy of Team-Assembly Systems: Understanding How People Use Technologies to Form Teams," *Proceedings of the ACM on Human-Computer Interaction* 4, no. CSCW2 (2020), https://doi.org/10.1145/3415252.

14. Farnaz Jahanbakhsh et al., "You Want Me to Work with Who?: Stakeholder Perceptions of Automated Team Formation in Project-based Courses," *Proceedings of the 2017 CHI Conference on Human Factors in Computing Systems*, Denver, 2017. Association for Computing Machinery.

15. Emily M. Hastings et al., "Composing Team Compositions: An Examination of Instructors' Current Algorithmic Team Formation Practices," *Proceedings of the ACM on Human-Computer Interaction* 7, no. CSCW2 (2023), https://doi.org/10.1145/3610096.

Chapter 13

1. Thomas W. Malone, Kevin Crowston, and George Arthur Herman, *Organizing Business Knowledge: The MIT Process Handbook* (The MIT Press, 2003).

Chapter 14

1. Simone Stolzoff, "After two years in stealth mode, the former head of HR at Google reveals his new startup," *Quartz*, October 8, 2018, https://qz.com/work/1415395/after-two-years-in-stealth-mode-the-former-head-of-hr-at-google-reveals-his-new-startup.

2. Sharon Zhou, Melissa Valentine, and Michael S. Bernstein, "In Search of the Dream Team: Temporally Constrained Multi-Armed Bandits for Identifying Effective Team Structures," *Proceedings of the 2018 CHI Conference on Human Factors in Computing Systems*, Montreal, Canada, 2018. Association for Computing Machinery.

3. Zhou, Valentine, and Bernstein, "In Search of the Dream Team."

4. Salehi and Bernstein, "Hive: Collective Design Through Network Rotation," 2.

5. Salehi and Bernstein, 17.

6. Salehi and Bernstein, 13.

7. Salehi and Bernstein, 13.

Chapter 15

1. Joon Sung Park et al., "Generative Agents: Interactive Simulacra of Human Behavior," in *Proceedings of the 36th Annual ACM Symposium on User Interface Software and Technology*, San Francisco, 2023. Association for Computing Machinery.

2. Park et al., "Generative Agents."

3. Park et al., "Generative Agents."

4. Anita Williams Woolley et al., "Evidence for a Collective Intelligence Factor in the Performance of Human Groups," *Science* 330, no. 6004 (2010), https://doi.org/10.1126/science.1193147.

5. Robert I. Sutton, *The No Asshole Rule: Building a Civilized Workplace and Surviving One That Isn't* (Grand Central Publishing, 2007).

6. K. Anders Ericsson, "Deliberate Practice and Acquisition of Expert Performance: A General Overview," *Academic Emergency Medicine* 15, no. 11 (2008), https://doi.org/10.1111/j.1553-2712.2008.00227.x.

7. Omar Shaikh et al., "Rehearsal: Simulating Conflict to Teach Conflict Resolution," in *Proceedings of the CHI Conference on Human Factors in Computing Systems*, Honolulu, HI, 2024. Association for Computing Machinery.

8. Anne L. Lytle, Jeanne M. Brett, and Debra L. Shapiro, "The Strategic Use of Interests, Rights, and Power to Resolve Disputes," *Negotiation Journal* 15, no. 1 (1999), https://doi.org/10.1111/j.1571-9979.1999.tb00178.x.

Chapter 16

1. John Mordechai Gottman and Robert Wayne Levenson, "The Timing of Divorce: Predicting When a Couple Will Divorce Over a 14-Year Period," *Journal of Marriage and Family* 62, no. 3 (2000), https://doi.org/10.1111/j.1741-3737.2000.00737.x.

2. Malte F. Jung, "Coupling Interactions and Performance: Predicting Team Performance from Thin Slices of Conflict," *Proceedings of the ACM on Human-Computer Interaction* 23, no. 3 (2016), https://doi.org/10.1145/2753767.

3. Mark E. Whiting et al., "Did It Have To End This Way? Understanding The Consistency of Team Fracture," *Proceedings of the ACM on Human-Computer Interaction* 3, no. CSCW (2019), https://doi.org/10.1145/3359311.

4. Jessica Nicole Cooperstein, "Initial Development of a Team Viability Measure," *DePaul University College of Science and Health Theses and Dissertations* 202 (2017).

5. Mark E. Whiting et al., "Parallel Worlds: Repeated Initializations of the Same Team to Improve Team Viability," *Proceedings of the ACM on Human-Computer Interaction* 4, no. CSCW1 (2020), https://doi.org/10.1145/3392877.

6. Katharina Lix et al., "Aligning Differences: Discursive Diversity and Team Performance," *Management Science* 68, no. 11 (2022), https://doi.org/10.1287/mnsc.2021.4274.

Chapter 17

1. Alan Blinder, "How Many US Jobs Might be Offshorable?," *World Economics* 10, no. 2 (2009): 41, https://EconPapers.repec.org/RePEc:wej:wldecn:376.

2. Lee et al., "Working with Machines: The Impact of Algorithmic and Data-Driven Management on Human Workers."

3. Gray and Suri, *Ghost Work: How to Stop Silicon Valley from Building a New Global Underclass.*

4. Aniket Kittur et al., "The Future of Crowd Work," *Proceedings of the 2013 Conference on Computer-Supported Cooperative Work* (ACM, 2013).

5. Min Kyung Lee et al., "Working with Machines: The Impact of Algorithmic and Data-Driven Management on Human Workers," *Proceedings of the 33rd Annual ACM Conference on Human Factors in Computing Systems*, Seoul, Republic of Korea, 2015. Association for Computing Machinery.

6. Ali Alkhatib, Michael Bernstein, and Margaret Levi, "Examining Crowd Work and Gig Work through the Historical Lens of Piecework," *Computer Science Department and CASBS Stanford University* (2017), https://doi.org/10.1145/3025453.3025974.

7. Gaikwad et al., "Boomerang: Rebounding the Consequences of Reputation Feedback on Crowdsourcing Platforms."

8. Snehalkumar 'Neil' Gaikwad et al., "Prototype Tasks: Improving Crowdsourcing Results through Rapid, Iterative Task Design," ArXiv, https://doi.org/10.48550/arXiv.1707.05645.

9. Pranav Rajpurkar et al., "Know What You Don't Know: Unanswerable questions for SQuAD," arXiv preprint, 2018, arXiv:1806.03822.

10. Niloufar Salehi et al., "We Are Dynamo: Overcoming Stalling and Friction in Collective Action for Crowd Workers," *Proceedings of the 33rd Annual ACM Conference*

on Human Factors in Computing Systems, Seoul, Republic of Korea, 2015. Association for Computing Machinery.

11. Mark E. Whiting, Grant Hugh, and Michael S. Bernstein, "Fair Work: Crowd Work Minimum Wage with One Line of Code," *Proceedings of the AAAI Conference on Human Computation and Crowdsourcing* 7, no. 1 (2019), https://doi.org/10.1609/hcomp.v7i1.5283.

12. Miranda Katz, "How an App Could Give Some Gig Workers a Safety Net," *Wired*, July 9, 2018, https://www.wired.com/story/how-an-app-could-give-some-gig-workers-a-safety-net/.

13. Ryo Suzuki et al., "Atelier: Repurposing Expert Crowdsourcing Tasks as Microinternships," *Proceedings of the 2016 CHI Conference on Human Factors in Computing Systems*, San Jose, CA, 2024. Association for Computing Machinery. https://doi.org/10.48550/arXiv.1602.06634.

14. Mark E. Whiting et al., "Crowd Guilds: Worker-Led Reputation and Feedback on Crowdsourcing Platforms," *Proceedings of the 20th ACM Conference on Computer Supported Cooperative Work and Social Computing*, Banff, Alberta, CA, 2016. Association for Computing Machinery.

15. Noam Scheiber (@noamscheiber), "Agree. Key is organizing workers on the platforms. Hollywood is all temp orgs. But unions are strong, wrkers do well," Twitter, July 13, 2017, https://x.com/noamscheiber/status/885532964498669568.

16. Niloufar Salehi et al., "We Are Dynamo."

17. "Freelance Forward 2023," Upwork, 2023, https://www.upwork.com/research/freelance-forward-2023-research-report.

18. Lawrence Lessig, *Code: Version 2.0*, 2nd ed. (SoHo Books, 2010).

Chapter 18

1. José María Barrero, Nicholas Bloom, and Steven J. Davis, "The Evolution of Work from Home," *Journal of Economic Perspectives* 37, no. 4 (2023), https://doi.org/10.1257/jep.37.4.23.

2. Emanuele Colonnelli et al., "Polarizing Corporations: Does Talent Flow to "Good" Firms?," Working Paper (2023).

3. G.F. Davis, *The Vanishing American Corporation: Navigating the Hazards of a New Economy* (Berrett-Koehler Publishers, 2016).

4. Ray Dalio, *Principles: Life and Work* (Simon and Schuster, 2017).

5. Yochai Benkler, *The Wealth of Networks: How Social Production Transforms Markets and Freedom* (Yale University Press, 2006).

6. "Team chat and channels with Slack," Slack, accessed 2024-06-02, https://slack.com/resources/using-slack/team-chat-and-channels-with-slack.

7. Clay Bavor, "Project Starline: Feel like you're there, together," *The Keyword (Google blog)*, May 18, 2021, https://blog.google/technology/research/project-starline/.

8. "How to have a Zoom meeting that is (almost) as good as being there," University of California, San Francisco, https://it.ucsf.edu/sites/it.ucsf.edu/files/zoom-best-practices.pdf.

9. Scott Kirsner, "Being There," *Fast Company*, January 1, 2006, https://www.fastcompany.com/54835/being-there.

10. Jim Hollan and Scott Stornetta, "Beyond Being There," *Proceedings of the SIGCHI Conference on Human Factors in Computing Systems*, Monterey, California, 1992. Association for Computing Machinery.

11. Rich Adams, "This site would suggest around 70–80ms latency between East/West coast US is typical (San Francisco to New York for example)," serverfault, April 30, 2010, https://serverfault.com/questions/137348/how-much-network-latency-is-typical-for-east-west-coast-usa#comment119149_137364.

12. Hollan and Stornetta, "Beyond Being There."

13. Frederick P. Brooks, Jr., *The Mythical Man-Month: Essays on Software Engineering*, (Addison-Wesley Publishing Company, 1995).

14. Jonathan Grudin, "Groupware and Social Dynamics: Eight Challenges for Developers," *Communications of the ACM* 37, no. 1 (1994).

15. National Research Council, *Continuing Innovation in Information Technology* (The National Academies Press, 2012), https://nap.nationalacademies.org/catalog/13427/continuing-innovation-in-information-technology.

16. *The Simpsons*, "Mr. Plow," season 4, episode 9, 1992.

Bibliography

Adams, Rich. "This Site Would Suggest around 70–80ms Latency between East/West Coast Us Is Typical (San Francisco to New York for Example)." *ServerFault* (2010).

Alkhatib, Ali, Michael Bernstein, and Margaret Levi. "Examining Crowd Work and Gig Work through the Historical Lens of Piecework." *Computer Science Department and CASBS Stanford University*, 2017. https://doi.org/10.1145/3025453.3025974.

Anders Ericsson, K. "Deliberate Practice and Acquisition of Expert Performance: A General Overview." *Academic Emergency Medicine* 15, no. 11 (2008): 988–994.

Barrero, José María, Nicholas Bloom, and Steven J. Davis. "The Evolution of Work from Home." *Journal of Economic Perspectives* 37, no. 4 (2023): 23–50.

Bavor, Clay. "Project Starline: Feel Like You're There, Together." The Keyword (Google blog), May 18, 2021.

Bechky, B. A. "Gaffers, Gofers, and Grips: Role-Based Coordination in Temporary Organizations." *Organization Science* 17, no. 1 (2006): 3–21.

Benkler, Yochai. *The Wealth of Networks: How Social Production Transforms Markets and Freedom*. Yale University Press, 2006.

Bigley, G. A., and K. H. Roberts. "The Incident Command System: High-Reliability Organizing for Complex and Volatile Task Environments." *Academy of Management Journal* 44, no. 6 (2001): 1281–1299.

Blinder, Alan. "How Many Us Jobs Might Be Offshorable?" *World Economics* 10, no. 2 (2009): 41–78.

Bohn, R. "From Art to Science in Manufacturing: The Evolution of Technological Knowledge." *Foundations and Trends in Technology, Information, and Operations Management* 1, no. 2 (2005): 1–82.

Brooks, Frederick P. *The Mythical Man-Month: Essays on Software Engineering*. Addison-Wesley, 1995.

The Simpsons. "Mr. Plow." Season 4, episode 9, 1992.

Chang, Jonathan P., Justin Cheng, and Cristian Danescu-Niculescu-Mizil. "Don't Let Me Be Misunderstood: Comparing Intentions and Perceptions in Online Discussions." Paper presented at The Web Conference 2020.

Coase, Ronald H. "The Nature of the Firm." *economica* 4, no. 16 (1937): 386–405.

Colonnelli, Emanuele, Timothy McQuade, Gabriel Ramos, Thomas Rauter, and Olivia Xiong. "Polarizing Corporations: Does Talent Flow to 'Good' Firms?" Working Paper (2023).

Colson, Eric. "Curiosity-Driven Data Science." *Harvard Business Review* (2018). https://hbr.org/2018/11/curiosity-driven-data-science.

Cooperstein, Jessica Nicole. "Initial Development of a Team Viability Measure." *College of Science and Health Theses and Dissertations* 202 (2017).

Council, National Research. *Continuing Innovation in Information Technology*. The National Academies Press, 2012. https://doi.org/10.17226/13427.

Dalio, Ray. *Principles: Life and Work*. Simon and Schuster, 2017.

Dastin, Jeffrey. "Insight—Amazon Scraps Secret AI Recruiting Tool That Showed Bias against Women." *Reuters*, October 10, 2018.

Davis, Andrew, director. *The Fugitive*. Warner Bros., 1993. 2 hr., 10 min.

Davis, G.F. *The Vanishing American Corporation: Navigating the Hazards of a New Economy*. Berrett-Koehler Publishers, 2016.

Davis, Steven J., R. Jason Faberman, and John C. Haltiwanger. "The Establishment-Level Behavior of Vacancies and Hiring." *Quarterly Journal of Economics* 128, no. 2 (2013).

Edmondson, A. *Teaming: How Organizations Learn, Innovate, and Compete in the Knowledge Economy*. Jossey-Bass, 2012.

Edmondson, Amy C. "Psychological Safety and Learning Behavior in Work Teams." *Administrative Science Quarterly* 44, no. 2 (1999): 350–383.

Edmondson, Amy C. "Teamwork on the Fly." *Harvard Business Review* 90, no. 4 (2012): 72–80.

Eyal, Gil. "For a Sociology of Expertise: The Social Origins of the Autism Epidemic." *American Journal of Sociology* 118, no. 4 (2013): 863–907.

Faraj, S., and Y. Xiao. "Coordination in Fast-Response Organizations." *Management Science* 52, no. 8 (2006): 1155–1169.

Filippas, Apostolos, John Joseph Horton, and Joseph Golden. "Reputation Inflation." Proceedings of the 2018 ACM Conference on Economics and Computation. Association for Computing Machinery. Ithaca, NY, 2018.

"Freelance Forward 2023." Upwork, 2023. https://www.upwork.com/research/freelance-forward-2023-research-report.

Gaikwad, S. S., D. Morina, A. Ginzberg, C. Mullings, S. Goyal, D. Gamage, C. Diemert, et al. "Boomerang: Rebounding the Consequences of Reputation Feedback on Crowdsourcing Platforms." Proceedings of the 29th Annual ACM Symposium on User Interface Software and Technology. Association for Computing Machinery. New York, 2016.

Gaikwad, Snehalkumar `Neil', Nalin Chhibber, Vibhor Sehgal, Alipta Ballav, Catherine A. Mullings, Ahmed Nasser, Angela Richmond-Fuller, et al. "Prototype Tasks: Improving Crowdsourcing Results through Rapid, Iterative Task Design." *Stanford Crowd Research Collective*. https://doi.org/10.48550/arXiv.1707.05645.

Gómez-Zará, Diego, Leslie A. DeChurch, and Noshir S. Contractor. "A Taxonomy of Team-Assembly Systems: Understanding How People Use Technologies to Form Teams." *Proceedings of the ACM on Human-Computer Interaction* 4, no. 181 (2020).

Gómez-Zará, Diego, Matthew Paras, Marlon Twyman, Jacqueline N. Lane, Leslie A. DeChurch, and Noshir S. Contractor. "Who Would You Like to Work With?" Proceedings of the 2019 CHI Conference on Human Factors in Computing Systems. Association for Computing Machinery. Glasgow, Scotland, 2019.

Gottman, John Mordechai, and Robert Wayne Levenson. "The Timing of Divorce: Predicting When a Couple Will Divorce over a 14-Year Period." *Journal of Marriage and Family* 62, no. 3 (2000): 737–745.

Gray, M.L., and S. Suri. *Ghost Work: How to Stop Silicon Valley from Building a New Global Underclass*. Harper Business, 2019.

Grudin, Jonathan. "Groupware and Social Dynamics: Eight Challenges for Developers." *Communications of the ACM* 37, no. 1 (1994): 92–105.

Gulati, R., and H. Singh. "The Architecture of Cooperation: Managing Coordination Costs and Appropriation Concerns in Strategic Alliances." [In English]. *Administrative Science Quarterly* 43, no. 4 (Dec 1998): 781–814.

Harris, Alexa M., Diego Gómez-Zará, Leslie A. DeChurch, and Noshir S. Contractor. "Joining Together Online: The Trajectory of Cscw Scholarship on Group Formation." *Proceedings of the ACM on Human-Computer Interaction* 3, no. 148 (2019).

Hastings, Emily M., Vidushi Ojha, Benedict V. Austriaco, Karrie Karahalios, and Brian P. Bailey. "Composing Team Compositions: An Examination of Instructors' Current Algorithmic Team Formation Practices." *Proceedings of the ACM on Human-Computer Interaction* 7, no. 305.

Heaphy, Emily D. "Repairing Breaches with Rules: Maintaining Institutions in the Face of Everyday Disruptions." *Organization Science* 24, no. 5 (2013): 1291–1315.

Hinds, Pamela J., and Diane E. Bailey. "Out of Sight, out of Sync: Understanding Conflict in Distributed Teams." *Organization Science* 14, no. 6 (2003): 615–632.

Hinds, Rebecca. "Knowledge Management in Remote First Companies." Working Paper. 2022.

Hollan, Jim, and Scott Stornetta. "Beyond Being There." Proceedings of the SIGCHI Conference on Human Factors in Computing Systems. Association for Computing Machinery. Monterey, California, 1992.

Hong, Lu, and Scott E. Page. "Groups of Diverse Problem Solvers Can Outperform Groups of High-Ability Problem Solvers." *Proceedings of the National Academy of Sciences* 101, no. 46 (2004): 16385–16389.

Irani, Lilly C, and M. Silberman. "Turkopticon: Interrupting Worker Invisibility in Amazon Mechanical Turk." *Proceedings of the SIGCHI Conference on Human Factors in Computing Systems*. Special Interest Group on Computer–Human Interaction. New York, 2013.

Iriondi, Roberto. "Amazon Scraps Secret AI Recruiting Tool That Showed Bias against Women." *Data Driven Investor* (Medium blog), October 10, 2018. https://medium.datadriveninvestor.com/amazon-scraps-secret-ai-recruiting-engine-that-showed-biases-against-women-995c505f5c6f.

Jahanbakhsh, Farnaz, Wai-Tat Fu, Karrie Karahalios, Darko Marinov, and Brian Bailey. "You Want Me to Work with Who?: Stakeholder Perceptions of Automated Team Formation in Project-Based Courses." 2017.

Jung, Malte F. "Coupling Interactions and Performance: Predicting Team Performance from Thin Slices of Conflict." *Proceedings of the ACM on Human-Computer Interaction*. 23, no. 3 (2016): Article 18.

Katz, Miranda. "How an App Could Give Some Gig Workers a Safety Net." *Wired*, July 9, 2010.

Kirsner, Scott. "Being There." *Fast Company*, January 1, 2006.

Kittur, Aniket, Jeffrey V Nickerson, Michael Bernstein, Elizabeth Gerber, Aaron Shaw, John Zimmerman, Matt Lease, and John Horton. "The Future of Crowd Work." *Proceedings of the 2013 Conference on Computer Supported Cooperative Work*. Association for Computing Machinery. New York, 2013.

Klein, K. J., J. C. Ziegert, A. P. Knight, and Y. Xiao. "Dynamic Delegation: Hierarchical, Shared and Deindividualized Leadership in Extreme Action Teams." *Administrative Science Quarterly* 51, no. 4 (Dec 2006): 590–621. https://doi.org/10.2189/asqu.51.4.590.

Kokkalis, Nicolas, Thomas Köhn, Carl Pfeiffer, Dima Chornyi, Michael S. Bernstein, and Scott R. Klemmer. "Emailvalet: Managing Email Overload through Private,

Accountable Crowdsourcing." Paper presented at the 2013 Conference on Computer Supported Cooperative Work. Association for Computing Machinery. New York, 2013.

Lee, Min Kyung, Daniel Kusbit, Evan Metsky, and Laura Dabbish. "Working with Machines: The Impact of Algorithmic and Data-Driven Management on Human Workers." *Proceedings of the 33rd Annual ACM Conference on Human Factors in Computing Systems*. Association for Computing Machinery. Seoul, Republic of Korea, 2015.

Lessig, Lawrence. *Code: Version 2.0*. 2nd ed. SoHo Books, 2010.

Liang, Diane Wei, Richard L Moreland, and Linda Argote. "Group Versus Individual Training and Group Performance: The Mediating Factor of Transactive Memory." *Personality and Social Psychology Bulletin* 21, no. 4 (1995): 384–393.

Lix, Katharina, Amir Goldberg, Sameer B. Srivastava, and Melissa A. Valentine. "Aligning Differences: Discursive Diversity and Team Performance." *Management Science* 68, no. 11 (2022): 8430–8448.

Lix, Katharina Lucia Maria. "Mixed-Method Approaches to Employment Relationships in Team-Based Online Gig Work." PhD Diss., Stanford University, 2021. https://purl.stanford.edu/rm124wf4080.

Lix, Katharina and Melissa A. Valentine. "When a Bot Scores Your Karma: Algorithmic Ranking Systems as Uncertainty Reducers in Platform Gig Work." Working Paper, Stanford University (2020).

Lu, Li, Y. Connie Yuan, and Poppy Lauretta McLeod. "Twenty-Five Years of Hidden Profiles in Group Decision Making: A Meta-Analysis." *Personality and Social Psychology Review* 16, no. 1 (2012): 54–75.

Lytle, Anne L., Jeanne M. Brett, and Debra L. Shapiro. "The Strategic Use of Interests, Rights, and Power to Resolve Disputes." *Negotiation Journal* 15, no. 1 (1999): 31–51.

Ma, Thomas, Michael S Bernstein, Ramesh Johari, and Nikhil Garg. "Balancing Producer Fairness and Efficiency Via Prior-Weighted Rating System Design." 2023. ArXiv preprint. https://doi.org/10.48550/arXiv.2207.04369.

Malone, Thomas W., Kevin Crowston, and George Arthur Herman. *Organizing Business Knowledge: The MIT Process Handbook*. The MIT Press, 2003.

Martin, David, Benjamin V. Hanrahan, Jacki O'Neill, and Neha Gupta. "Being a Turker." *Proceedings of the 17th ACM Conference on Computer Supported Cooperative Work and Social Computing*. Association for Computing Machinery. Baltimore, Maryland, 2014.

McInnis, Brian, Dan Cosley, Chaebong Nam, and Gilly Leshed. "Taking a Hit: Designing around Rejection, Mistrust, Risk, and Workers' Experiences in Amazon Mechanical Turk." *Proceedings of the 2016 CHI Conference on Human Factors in*

Computing Systems. Association for Computing Machinery. San Jose, California, 2016.

Meyerson, D., K. E. Weick, and R.M. Kramer. "Swift Trust and Temporary Groups." In *Trust in Organizations: Frontiers of Theory and Research*, edited by R.M. Kramer and T.E. Tyler. Sage, 1996.

Nehrlich, Eric. "Plans and Situated Actions, by Lucy Suchman." *Eric Nehrlich, Unrepentant Generalist*, September 6, 2005. https://www.nehrlich.com/blog/2005/09/06/plans-and-situated-actions-by-lucy-suchman/.

Page, Scott E. *The Difference: How the Power of Diversity Creates Better Groups, Firms, Schools, and Societies*. Princeton University Press, 2008.

Pan, Christina A., Sahil Yakhmi, Tara P. Iyer, Evan Strasnick, Amy X. Zhang, and Michael S. Bernstein. "Comparing the Perceived Legitimacy of Content Moderation Processes: Contractors, Algorithms, Expert Panels, and Digital Juries." *Proceedings of the ACM on Human-Computer Interaction* 6, no. 82 (2022): 1–31.

Park, Joon Sung, Joseph O'Brien, Carrie Jun Cai, Meredith Ringel Morris, Percy Liang, and Michael S. Bernstein. "Generative Agents: Interactive Simulacra of Human Behavior." *Proceedings of the 36th Annual ACM Symposium on User Interface Software and Technology*. Association for Computing Machinery. San Francisco, CA, 2023.

Pirolli, P. *Information Foraging Theory: Adaptive Interaction with Information*. Human Technology Interaction Series. Oxford University Press, 2009.

Rahman, Hatim A. "The Invisible Cage: Workers' Reactivity to Opaque Algorithmic Evaluations." *Administrative Science Quarterly* 66, no. 4 (2021): 945–988.

Rahman, Hatim A., and Melissa A. Valentine. "How Managers Maintain Control through Collaborative Repair: Evidence from Platform-Mediated 'Gigs'." *Organization Science* 32, no. 5 (2021).

Rajpurkar, Pranav, Robin Jia, and Percy Liang. "Know What You Don't Know: Unanswerable Questions for Squad." Working Paper, Stanford University. 2018.

Reagans, R., L. Argote, and D. Brooks. "Individual Experience and Experience Working Together: Predicting Learning Rates from Knowing Who Knows What and Knowing How to Work Together." *Management Science* 51, no. 6 (Jun 2005): 869–881. https://doi.org/10.1287/mnsc.1050.0366.

Retelny, Daniela, Michael S. Bernstein, and Melissa A Valentine. "No Workflow Can Ever Be Enough: How Crowdsourcing Workflows Constrain Complex Work." *Proceedings of the ACM on Human-Computer Interaction* 1, no. CSCW (2017): 1–23.

Rhymer, Jen. "Location-Independent Organizations: Designing Collaboration across Space and Time." *Administrative Science Quarterly* 68, no. 1 (2023): 1–43.

Bibliography

Salehi, Niloufar and Michael S. Bernstein. "Hive: Collective Design through Network Rotation." *Proceedings of the ACM on Human-Computer Interaction* 2, no. CSCW (November 2018): 151.

Salehi, Niloufar, Lilly Irani, Michael Bernstein, Ali Alkhatib, Eva Ogbe, Kristy Milliland, and Clickhappier. "We Are Dynamo: Overcoming Stalling and Friction in Collective Action for Crowd Workers." *Proceedings of the 33rd Annual ACM Conference on Human Factors in Computing Systems*. Association for Computing Machinery. Seoul, Republic of Korea, 2015.

Salehi, Niloufar, Andrew McCabe, Melissa Valentine, and Michael Bernstein. "Huddler: Convening Stable and Familiar Crowd Teams Despite Unpredictable Availability." *Proceedings of the 2017 ACM Conference on Computer Supported Cooperative Work and Social Computing*. Association for Computing Machinery. Portland, Oregon, 2017.

San Francisco, University of California. "How to Have a Zoom Meeting That Is (Almost) as Good as Being There." https://it.ucsf.edu/how-to/how-have-zoom-meeting-almost-good-being-there.

Scheiber, Noam. "The Pop-up Employer: Build a Team, Do the Job, Say Goodbye." *New York Times*, July 12, 2017.

Scheiber, Noam (@noamscheiber). "Agree. Key Is Organizing Workers on the Platforms. Hollywood Is All Temp Orgs. But Unions Are Strong, Wrkers Do Well." Twitter, July 13, 2017. https://x.com/noamscheiber/status/885532964498669568.

Shaikh, Omar, Valentino Emil Chai, Michele Gelfand, Diyi Yang, and Michael S. Bernstein. "Rehearsal: Simulating Conflict to Teach Conflict Resolution." *Proceedings of the CHI Conference on Human Factors in Computing Systems*. Association for Computing Machinery. Honolulu, HI, 2024.

Silberman, M. S., B. Tomlinson, R. LaPlante, J. Ross, L. Irani, and A. Zaldivar. "Responsible Research with Crowds: Pay Crowdworkers at Least Minimum Wage." *Communications of the ACM* 61, no. 3 (2018): 39–41.

Simon, Herbert A. "The Architecture of Complexity." *Proceedings of the American Philosophical Society* 106, no. 6 (Dec. 12 1962): 467–482.

"Team Chat and Channels with Slack." Slack. Accessed 2024-06-02, https://slack.com/resources/using-slack/team-chat-and-channels-with-slack.

Soper, Spencer. "Fired by Bot at Amazon: 'It's You against the Machine'." *Bloomberg*, June 28, 2021. https://www.bloomberg.com/news/features/2021-06-28/fired-by-bot-amazon-turns-to-machine-managers-and-workers-are-losing-out.

Stolzoff, Simone. "After Two Years in Stealth Mode, the Former Head of HR at Google Reveals His New Startup." *Quartz*, October 8, 2018. https://qz.com/work/1415395

/after-two-years-in-stealth-mode-the-former-head-of-hr-at-google-reveals-his-new-startup.

Suchman, Lucy A. *Plans and Situated Actions: The Problem of Human-Machine Communication*. Cambridge University Press, 1987.

Sutton, Bob. "Hierarchy Is Good. Hierarchy Is Essential. And Less Isn't Always Better." Stanford Technology Ventures Program, April 17, 2016. https://ecorner.stanford.edu/articles/hierarchy-is-good-hierarchy-is-essential-and-less-isnt-always-better/.

Sutton, Robert L. *Good Boss, Bad Boss: How to Be the Best . . . And Learn from the Worst*. Grand Central Publishing, 2012.

———. *The No Asshole Rule: Building a Civilized Workplace and Surviving One That Isn't*. Grand Central Publishing, 2007.

Suzuki, Ryo, Niloufar Salehi, Michelle S. Lam, Juan C. Marroquin, and Michael S. Bernstein. "Atelier: Repurposing Expert Crowdsourcing Tasks as Micro-Internships." *Proceedings of the 2016 CHI Conference on Human Factors in Computing Systems*. Association for Computing Machinery. New York, 2016. https://doi.org/10.48550/arXiv.1602.06634.

Valentine, Melissa. "When Equity Seems Unfair: The Role of Justice Enforceability in Temporary Team Coordination." *Academy of Management Journal* 61, no. 6 (2018): 2081–2105.

Valentine, Melissa A. "Renegotiating Spheres of Obligation: The Role of Hierarchy in Organizational Learning." *Administrative Science Quarterly* 63, no. 3 (2018).

Valentine, Melissa A., Steven M. Asch, and Esther Ahn. "Who Pays the Cancer Tax? Patients' Narratives in a Movement to Reduce Their Invisible Work." *Organization Science* 34, no. 4 (2023): 1400–1421.

Valentine, M. A., and A. C. Edmondson. "Team Scaffolds: How Mesolevel Structures Enable Role-Based Coordination in Temporary Groups." *Organization Science* 26, no. 2 (2015 2015): 405–422.

Valentine, Melissa A., Daniela Retelny, Alexandra To, Negar Rahmati, Tulsee Doshi, and Michael S. Bernstein. "Flash Organizations: Crowdsourcing Complex Work by Structuring Crowds as Organizations." *Proceedings of the 2017 CHI Conference on Human Factors in Computing Systems*. Denver, 2017.

Wageman, Ruth, J. Richard Hackman, and Erin Lehman. "Team Diagnostic Survey: Development of an Instrument." *The Journal of Applied Behavioral Science* 41, no. 4 (2005): 373–398.

Webb, Marissa. "Selective Attention Test." YouTube video, 5:12, uploaded January 11, 2018. https://youtu.be/_bnnmWYI0lM.

Bibliography

Whiting, Mark E., Allie Blaising, Chloe Barreau, Laura Fiuza, Nik Marda, Melissa Valentine, and Michael S. Bernstein. "Did It Have to End This Way? Understanding the Consistency of Team Fracture." *Proceedings of the ACM on Human-Computer Interaction* 3, no. 209 (2019): 1–23.

Whiting, Mark E., Dilrukshi Gamage, Aaron Gilbee, Snehal Gaikwad, Shirish Goyal, Alipta Ballav, Dinesh Majeti, et al. "Crowd Guilds: Worker-Led Reputation and Feedback on Crowdsourcing Platforms." *Proceedings of the 20th ACM Conference on Computer Supported Cooperative Work and Social Computing*. Portland, Oregon, 2017.

Whiting, Mark E., Irena Gao, Michelle Xing, N'godjigui Junior Diarrassouba, Tonya Nguyen, and Michael S. Bernstein. "Parallel Worlds: Repeated Initializations of the Same Team to Improve Team Viability." *Proceedings of the ACM on Human-Computer Interaction* 4, no. 67 (2020).

Whiting, Mark E., Grant Hugh, and Michael S. Bernstein. "Fair Work: Crowd Work Minimum Wage with One Line of Code." *Proceedings of the AAAI Conference on Human Computation and Crowdsourcing* 7, no. 1 (2019): 197–206.

Winter, Shannon. "A Product Marketer Walks into a Marketing Analytics Team." LinkedIn, November 21, 2019, https://www.linkedin.com/pulse/product-marketer-walks-marketing-analytics-team-shannon-winter/.

Woolley, Anita Williams, Christopher F. Chabris, Alex Pentland, Nada Hashmi, and Thomas W. Malone. "Evidence for a Collective Intelligence Factor in the Performance of Human Groups." *Science* 330, no. 6004 (2010): 686–688.

Wuchty, S., B. F. Jones, and B. Uzzi. "The Increasing Dominance of Teams in Production of Knowledge." *Science* 316, no. 5827 (2007): 1036–1039.

Zhou, Sharon, Melissa Valentine, and Michael S. Bernstein. "In Search of the Dream Team: Temporally Constrained Multi-Armed Bandits for Identifying Effective Team Structures." *Proceedings of the 2018 CHI Conference on Human Factors in Computing Systems*. Association for Computing Machinery. Montreal, Canada, 2018.

Index

Note: Page numbers in italics refer to figures; underlined page numbers refer to tables.

A/B tests, 141
Accenture, 6, 11, 37, 71
Accreditation, 175–176
Adaptation
  bottom-up, 71–72
  hierarchies and, 75–83
  overview of, 55–61
  through software, 63–74
  top-down, 72–73
Adaptive capability, 52
Agrawal, Niti, 81
Algorithmic ratings, 104, 105–112.
    See also Karma scores; Reputation
    scores/ratings
Alia, 174–175
Alkhatib, Ali, 172, 174
Amazon, 40
Amazon Mechanical Turk, 23, 41, 124,
    144, 148, 163, 169, 174, 177
Appen, 23
Application model, 41–42
Application programming interfaces
    (APIs), 7
Artella, 6–7, 11, 15
Artificial intelligence
  data requirements and, 187–188
  designing flash teams with, 129–135
  development of, 188–189

experts on, 23
flash team simulations and, 151–157
future of management and, 116–117
hiring and, 115–127, *122*, <u>123</u>, *125*
improving teams with, 137–149
judgments of, 112
objectives and, 117–123
perils of team recruitment based on,
    126–127
predicting outcomes with, 159–165
Asana, 68, 70
Assembly experiments, 124, 126
Assumptions, 56
A.Team, 11, 15, 26, 40, 43, 168–169
Atlassian, 25, 35
Attentional challenge, 59
Auditable decision trails, 35
Availability, 119, 124, 126

Backstage repair, 99–100
Bansal, Lokesh, 18
Bellcore, 183
Benefits, portable, 174–175, 179
Benkler, Yochai, 183
Bezos, Jeff, 177
Biases, 59, 60
Biederman, Rob, 105, 167
Blum, Daniela Retelny, 4, 37

Bock, Laszlo, 139, 140
Borland, John, 139
Branch-and-merge method, 67, 69–70
Branches, 66
Brooks, Fred, 186
Brown, Sarah, 42
B12, 11, 103–104, 105
Bunny Studio, 22
Business experts, 20

Cameo, 14, 20
Cao, Hancheng, 161
Career ladders, 172
Catalant, 11, 13, 15, 20, 43, 105, 167
Change
   amount of, 71
   hierarchies and, 85–91
   networks of managers and, 88–90
   preparing for, 51–52
ChatGPT, 155, 157, 188–189
Clickworker, 23
Client vision, 80–82
Client voice, 103–112
Closed-loop communication, 53
CloudDevs, 18
Coase, Ronald, 7–8
Codewords, 144
Coercive control, 95–96
Collaborative repair, 93–102
Communication
   divergent, 164–165
   networks of managers and, 86–89
   pitfalls regarding, 101–102
   protocols for, 53
   statements of work and, 81–82
   town halls and, 103–104
Community support, 103–105
Compliance, 73–74
Computing Research Association, 188
Connecting the dots, 88–90
Coordination software, 10–12
Cost, individual objectives and, 118

Creative writing/video experts, 20–21, *21*, 22–23
Criticism, coupling with praise, 97–98
Crowd guilds, 175–176
Crowd Research Collective, 176
Crowdsourcing, 57
Crowston, Kevin, 135
Cultivate, 139–140

Daemo, 173
Dalio, Ray, 183
Data annotation services, 23
Data requirements, 187–188
Data science experts, 23
Davis, Jerry, 8
Declines, 122
Deliberate practice, 155
Design experts, 18–20, *19*
Diamantopoulos, Chris, 14
Dickey, Roger, 39, 42, 54, 130–131
Disability leave, 174
Disaster response crews, 28
Disputes, threatening formal, 96
Diversity, 119–120
Division of labor, 59
Documentation, 34–36, 61, 76, 82
DreamTeam software, 141, *142*, *145*
DreamWorks, 183
Dribble, 20
Dropbox, 35
Dyer, Taurean, 11, 37, 98–99

Economic floor, guaranteed, 170
Economic Security Project, 170
Editing source code, 66–68, 70
Edmondson, Amy, 46, 60
Elastic organizations, 184, 186
Employee morale, 172–173
Employees versus independent contractors, 179
Empowered autonomous decision-making, 35
EMS Trauma Report Team, 71–72, *72*, 73

Index

Enterprise Workshop Planning Portal, 71, 72, 73
ER teams, 28, 29–30, 45, 53–54, 78
Etsy, 24
"Exact Instructions Challenge," 56
Experience, lack of, 171–172
Expert abundance, 13–14, 24–26, 184
Experts, curated pool of, 42–43
EY, 6

Fair Care Labs, 174–175
Fair Work, 174
Familiarity, 119, 124, 126
FastCompany, 183
Feedback, task-focused, 97
Film crews, 27–28, 51
Finance experts, 20
Firefox, 147
Fiverr, 15
Flash Hub, 11
Flash team libraries, 130–135, 145
Flash teams
  abilities of, 184
  adaptation and, 55–61, 63–74
  AI hiring and, 115–127
  barriers to use of, 9–10
  building healthy ecosystems for, 167–180
  collaborative repair and, 93–102
  coordination software for, 10–12
  description of, 4–5
  designing with AI, 129–135
  example of use of, 3–4
  hierarchies and, 75–83, 85–91
  hiring and onboarding tactics, 37–44
  implications of use of, 7–8
  improving, 137–149
  predicting outcomes of, 159–165
  role clarity and, 27–36
  simulations of, 151–157
  team behaviors and, 45–54
  uses for, 5–7

  worker voice and client voice and, 103–112
Foster, Natalie, 170
Foundry
  hiring and, 17, 38, 42, 115
  onboarding and, 47, *48*, *49*, *50*
  overview of, 10–12
  pull requests and, *68*, 70
  role orientation and, 65
  team structure and, 31
Freed, Joseph, 139
Freelancer (platform), 18
Freelance workers, 8
Fugitive, The, 76–77

Gelfand, Michele, 155
Generative agents, 152, 154
Ghost Work (Gray and Suri), 169
Gig economy, 15, 169, 170–173, 176, 179
Gigster
  automation and, 11
  flash team movement and, 6, 39
  hiring models and, 42–43
  karma scores and, 110–111, 118
  launching and, 46–47
  role foraging and, 32
  software development and, 17–18, 51
  study involving, 78, 82, 164
Git, 66
GitHub, 35, 66–67, 70, 133
GitHub Projects, 70
Gómez-Zará, Diego, 126
Google DeepMind, 11
Google Sheets, 70
Gottman, John, 160
Gottman, Julie, 160
Gray, Mary, 169
Greedy algorithms, 121
Grudin's Paradox, 188
Guarantee, The (Foster), 170

Hackman, Richard, 52
Handoffs, 75–76, 83

Hastings, Emily, 126
Health care insurance, 174
Hidden profile exercise, 60
Hierarchies, 64, 75–83, 85–91, 132–133
Hinds, Pamela, 101
Hiring, artificial intelligence and, 115–127, *122*, <u>123</u>, *125*
Hiring models, 40–42
Hiring tactics, 37–44
Hollan, Jim, 183–184
Horton, John, 107
HourlyNerd, 6
Humu, 139–140

Ideation tasks, 164
Incubator platform, 162–164
Indeed, 24
Independent contractors, employees versus, 179
Individual objectives, 117–119
Information flow, 82–83
Institutional Review Boards (IRBs), 177
Instructions, full, 55–57
Interests–Rights–Power framework, 155, *156*, 157
Internships, 175
Interpersonal skills, AI simulations and, 155, *156*, 157
IQ, team objectives and, 119

Jahanbakhsh, Farnaz, 126
Job postings, 39–40
Job rotations, 25
Joint responsibility, 54
J.P. Morgan, 6
Jung, Malte, 160

Karma scores, 110–111, 118. *See also* Algorithmic ratings; Reputation scores/ratings

Large language models, 152, *153*, 154
Launching, 46–51, 162–164
Leadership, impact of, 75–76

Learning and development (L&D) systems, 138–139
Lee, Min Kyung, 106
Lego metaphor, 131, *132*
Levi, Margaret, 172
LinkedIn, 24
Linking pin positions, 86
Lix, Katharina, 78–79, 82, 110, 164–165
Location-independent organizations (LIOs), 35–36

Malone, Tom, 135
Marcus, Adam, 103–105
Matchmaking model, 41
McInnis, Brian, 102
Merging, 67
Meta, 25
Metti, Maxx, 40, 43
Micro-internships, 175
Monster, 24
Morale, 172–173
Mozilla, 147–148
Multi-armed bandit, 141

National Domestic Workers Alliance (NDWA), 174
Network rotation, 146–148, *146*, *147*
Networks of managers, 86–89
No-shows, 122
Nudge systems, 137, 138–140

Objectives, 117–124, 126–127
Ocean's Eleven, 28, 34
Olaosebikan, Debo, 39, 46, 54
Onboarding, 37–44, 46–51
On-demand experts, 184, 186–187
Online labor markets. *See also individual platforms*
 algorithmic ratings and, 105–106
 experts available on, 17–23
 overview of, 14–17
Opaque rating scores, 108–109
Open calls, 40–42
Open source software, 178

Index

Orchestra, 11, 103
Organizational charts, 64
Organizational design, 182–183
Organizational learning, 137–138, 140
Organizational theory, 138
Organization of online workers, 176–178
Outcome measurements, 133
Ouzan, Raphael, 26, 168–169
Overhauls, large-scale, 73

Page, Larry, 91
Page, Scott, 119–120
Park, Joon, 151, 152
Payment, threatening, 96
Payment protections, 174
Perceptyx, 138–140
Performance, rewarding team, 52
Petitti, Pat, 13, 43, 105
Piecework payment, 172–173
Pinto, Lisa, 29
Pitfalls, common, 100–101
Platform Worker Directive, 179
Policy, possible developments in, 178–180
Praise, coupling with criticism, 97–98
Principles (Dalio), 183
Process Knowledge Spectrum, 60
Project managers (PMs)
    client vision and, 80–82
    importance of, 78–79
    information and resources flow, 82–83
    role of, 79–80
Project Starline, 183
Prosocial behaviors, 52
Prototype tasks, 173
Pull requests, 67–70, *68*, 71

Rahman, Hatim, 94, 108
Railroads, organization and, 182
Rating inflation, 106–108
Ratings, threatening, 96
React web applications, 18

Repair work, 87, 93–102
Reputation scores. *See* Karma scores
Reputation scores/ratings, 16, 106, 118.
    See also Algorithmic ratings
Requests, 67
Residual complexity, 79–80
Resource flow, 82–83
Responsibility, shared, 98–99
Retirement savings, 174
Review, 67
Rhymer, Jen, 35
Role-based simulations, 151–152, *153*, 154
Role-based software, 65–66
Role-based teaming, 29, 52–54
Role clarity, 27–36, 83
Role foraging, 32–34, 47
Role orientation, 65
Role structure, defining, 30–32

Salehi, Niloufar, 124, 145–146
Samasource, 23
Scale AI, 23
Scheiber, Noam, 77, 176
Search engines, 135
Secondments, 25
Self-employed classification policies, 179
Seshardri, Sri, 88
Shaikh, Omar, 155
Shared responsibility, 98–99
Shpak, Anna, 6
Sick leave, 174
Silberman, M. Six, 101
Single source of truth (SSOT) documentation, 35, 76, 82
Slack, 183
Soft skills, 155, 157
Software development, 17–18
Source code, 66–68, 70
SQuAD 2.0, 173
Stage 4 Solutions, 81
Stanford Crowd Research Collective, 173

Statements of work (SOW), 81–82
Stochastic searches, 121–122
Stornetta, Scott, 183–184
Strategic directions, new, 73–74
Strategy experts, 20
Suri, Sid, 169
Surman, Kate, 88, 89
Sutton, Bob, 90–91
Suzuki, Ryo, 175

Talent clouds, 42
Task blocks, 132, 133
Task-focused feedback, 97
TaskRabbit, 24
Task reconfigurations, 73
Team behaviors, 45–54, 64, 159–162
Team design, client vision and, 80–82
Team fracture scores, 161
TeamHub, 133
Teaming behaviors, recognizing, 52
Team learning, 137
Team membership, evolving, 145–148
Team objectives, 117–118, 119–120
Team structures, 140–145, *142*, *143*, *145*
Temporary teams, 46
Theory of the firm, 7
Time zone overlap, 120
Tools, shared, 53
Town halls, 103–105
Trampoline capitalism, 170
Transparency, 75, 82
True Story Gaming Team, 71, 73
Trusted experts, 184, 187

Underpayment, 101, 174
Upwork
    algorithmic ratings and, 106–107, 108
    author's use of, 19–20, 22
    collaborative repair and, 94
    experts available on, 15, 20
    flash team movement and, 8
    formal disputes and, 96
    freelance statistics from, 178
    hierarchies and, 80
    hiring models and, 41, 42
    job postings and, 39
    micro-internships and, 175
    minimum wage on, 101
    payment protections and, 174
    role clarity and, 31
    search interface for, *16*
    software development and, 17–18
    workflow and, 57
    work of, 104

Vanishing Corporation, The (Davis), 8
Version control, 66–67, 69–70
Vetted panels, 40–42
Voice Bunny, 22

Wages, fair, 174
Wage theft, 101, 171, 174, 180
We Are Dynamo, 176–178
Weighting objectives, 120–121, *122*, <u>123</u>
We Work Remotely, 18
Whiting, Mark, 161, 162, 174
Wikipedia, 104
Winograd, Terry, 20, *21*, 22
Woolley, Anita, 119
Workana, 18
Worker voice, 103–112
Workflow
    adaptation and, 57–58
    roles versus, 65
Work-from-home arrangements, 181–182
Workspaces, shared, 53

Yang, Diyi, 155

Zhang, Amy X., 112
Zhou, Sharon, 141